Today's Titanic

Today's
Titanic

She's bigger. She's more seductive.
She's way more lethal.

Lyndell P. Enns

authorHOUSE®

AuthorHouse™
1663 Liberty Drive
Bloomington, IN 47403
www.authorhouse.com
Phone: 1-800-839-8640

Published by AuthorHouse 4/12/2013

ISBN: 978-1-4817-3497-4 (sc)
ISBN: 978-1-4817-3496-7 (hc)
ISBN: 978-1-4817-3702-9 (e)
Library of Congress Control Number: 2013905814

Unless indicated otherwise, Scripture quotations are taken from the
Amplified® Bible, Copyright © 1954, 1958, 1962, 1964, 1965, 1987 by The
Lockman Foundation . Used by permission. (www.Lockman.org)

Scripture quotations marked (NIV) are taken from THE HOLY BIBLE, NEW
INTERNATIONAL VERSION®, NIV® Copyright © 1973, 1978, 1984, 2011
by Biblica, Inc.™ Used by permission. All rights reserved worldwide.

Scripture quotations marked (NKJV) are taken from the New King James Version.
Copyright © 1982 by Thomas Nelson, Inc. Used by permission. All rights reserved.

Scripture quotations marked (NLT) are taken from the Holy Bible, New Living Translation,
copyright © 1996, 2004, 2007 by Tyndale House Foundation. Used by permission of
Tyndale House Publishers, Inc., Carol Stream, Illinois 60188. All rights reserved.

Scripture quotations marked (NET) are taken from the NET Bible® copyright ©1996-2006
by Biblical Studies Press, L.L.C., www.bible.org, Used by permission. All rights reserved.

*With deep appreciation to my parents
Henry and Luella who taught me to trust the Word*

Table of Contents

Chapter 1

TODAY'S TITANIC

When Titanic, the 'unsinkable ship' sank, *over fifteen hundred people* lost their lives. Many of them drowned while swimming near the lifeboats in the lethally cold water just after Titanic went down. For twenty awful minutes, those in the lifeboats were horrified to hear from the drowning people, "every possible emotion of human fear, despair, agony, fierce resentment and blind anger." These gut wrenching sounds were mingled with "notes of infinite surprise, as though each one were saying, 'How is it possible that this awful thing is happening to me? That I should be caught in this death trap?' " [1,2]

Yet just four hours earlier, when the stewards began ordering the passengers to put on their lifebelts, many passengers treated the order as a joke. Some set about playing an impromptu game of soccer with the ice chunks from the iceberg that were strewn across the foredeck. [1,3] At first, few passengers were even willing to board the lifeboats.[1,4] They were still confident that the Titanic was unsinkable!

But why did the 'unsinkable' Titanic sink?

She sank for one overarching reason...*people were in a stupor of false security--an overconfident sense of safety.* Take Captain E. J. Smith for example. He had said before the voyage, "I cannot imagine any condition which would cause a ship to founder. Modern shipbuilding has gone beyond that." [1,5] And so, he ignored seven iceberg warnings. One man

1

was so seduced by the strength and grandeur of the Titanic, he said, "God Himself couldn't sink this ship." [6,7]

They thought they were unsinkable...entirely secure. But it was precisely this *false sense of safety* that caused their demise because it kept them from carefully considering and acting on the real facts.

Today, there is another Titanic. It's far bigger, far more seductive, and far more lethal. It's a ship with innumerable passengers, who all have one thing in common—they think of themselves as Christians.

As Christians, it's easy to be riding on today's massive spiritual Titanic, feeling safe and heaven bound, even if we aren't heaven bound at all. Our over confident sense of safety is increased by seeing those around us on our 'Christian' ship, living and thinking just about the same as we do. Our false sense of security often keeps us from carefully considering and acting on the real facts, so we ignore the iceberg warnings all around us. We resist getting off the Titanic even after being warned. Unknowingly, I did this for years.

This book is an iceberg warning. Some Christians will ignore this warning—confident that all is well with their eternal ship. The more religious and church-going you are, and the longer you've been a Christian, the greater that temptation will be, because you are already so very confident in your ship. But there will be others who will stop and carefully consider the surprising facts that are gathered here in this easy-to-read book, and by acting on them, may well save their lives for eternity.

Consider for a moment, that key church-leaders including Billy Graham, believe that the great majority of people who attend 'Bible believing' churches are lost![8] A.W. Tozer said, "It is my opinion that tens of thousands of people, if not millions, have been brought into some kind of religious experience by accepting Christ, and they have not been saved."[9] But most surprising and significant, is the warning that *Jesus himself* gives about those who think they are Christians, when they aren't. We'll look at His words in the very next chapter.

Recently, a godly woman shared a vision with me, where she had seen droves of 'Christians' walking headlong with confidence, following their priests and pastors, but they were walking right off a cliff into a great black chasm. The woman could barely speak from emotion when she heard about the book you are reading right now, because this book explains exactly how and why such a tragedy is happening to millions of 'Christians' today.

Don't continue to read this book unless you are prepared to discover the deceptions that have slipped into Catholic, Protestant, Orthodox and Christian circles generally—deceptions which keep many people hoping and thinking they are heaven bound, when according to God's own words, they are not.

Most importantly, you will discover where to find these warning words of God, so you can read them for yourself in your own Bible, before it's too late to do something about them.

1. Wikipedia contributors. "Sinking of the RMS Titanic." *Wikipedia, The Free Encyclopedia.* Wikipedia, The Free Encyclopedia, 11 May. 2012. Web. 12 May. 2012.
2. Bartlett, W.B. (2011). Titanic: *9 Hours to Hell, the Survivors' Story.* Stroud, Gloucestershire: Amberley Publishing, 199-200.
3. Barczewski, Stephanie (2006). *Titanic: A Night Remembered.* London: Continuum International Publishing Group, 20.
4. Lord, Walter (1976). *A Night to Remember.* London: Penguin Books, 73-74.
5. Barczewski, Stephanie (2006). *Titanic: A Night Remembered.* London: Continuum International Publishing Group, 13.
6. David E. Pratte, "Lessons from the Titanic", 1999, May 16, 2012. http://www.gospelway.com/christianlife/titanic_lessons.php
7. Unsinkable": The Full Story of the RMS Titanic, by Daniel Allen Butler, 39.
8. Washer, Paul. "Shocking Message." Sermon on Heart Cry Films. 2002. YouTube. 28 October 2011.
9. Comfort, Ray. "True and False Conversion." Sermon. 2006. livingwaters.com. 21 October 2011.

Chapter 2

WHO?—ME?

I f you hope to get into heaven after you die, then you are like most Christians who have this same hope. But think again. You are about to see clear evidence in the Bible that many unsuspecting 'Christians' will actually go to hell instead.

"Christians in hell?" you ask. "Exactly who could this be referring to?"

The truth is, many who believe in Jesus, will at the end of their lives hear the most horrific, shocking, heart-sinking words ever, from Jesus Himself. They will be the words, "I never knew you; depart from Me, you who act wickedly [disregarding My commands]" (Matthew 7:23). And down to hell they will go.

These are people who had 'believed in Jesus' and called Him "Lord!"

Yes. You read correctly. *They had 'believed in Jesus' and called Jesus their Lord.* No doubt many of these had gone to church, confessed their sins, and even been baptized. No doubt many had prayed regularly and read their Bible. In fact the Bible says many had even been active in church ministries like preaching and healing. No doubt some had led ministries and others had even gone overseas to do the work of the church. Others had simply lived a life that seemed decent and good compared to most other people they knew in church. But then, to these who called Jesus "Lord, Lord," come the shocking and revealing words from Jesus Himself, "I never knew you; depart from Me, you who act wickedly [disregarding My commands]," (Matthew 7:21-23).

So, as surprising as it sounds, there is a faith in Jesus Christ that leads to hell...a false faith. Jesus warns us of this kind of faith all through the Bible, and you are about to discover exactly what this deceptive faith is, and what it looks like today in its many common forms.

But what is very scary, is how many Catholics and Protestants and Orthodox Christians are following this faith today without realizing it. It is an unbelievably common deception that has permeated much of the church, partly because many church leaders are choosing to teach people what they prefer to hear. These leaders teach a popular and comfortable, politically correct message that preserves their popularity, their pay cheque, and their position, when they ought to be teaching the truth instead.

Moreover, many of these leaders are unaware of the deception they teach because they are simply passing along what they have been taught by their own teachers. They haven't surveyed God's Word for the purpose of sorting out for themselves what is truth and what is merely tradition. That's dangerous because some traditions can be good, while others are opposite to the truth. As a result, both truth and lies have been passed on as truth, and the deception has compounded to become a worldwide epidemic in Christianity today.

Dennis James Kennedy of Evangelism Explosion said, "The vast majority of people who are members of churches in America today are not Christians. I say that without the slightest fear of contradiction. I base it on empirical evidence of twenty-four years of examining thousands of people."[1]

We start to see how it is possible that many who call Jesus their Lord, could be so deceived and off track that Jesus will actually deny knowing them and send them to destruction. The size of this deceptive infection is so big, so broad and so bad, that it is nearly certain you are affected in some way, directly or indirectly, whether you know it or not.

But how would you know it, if you *were*? The problem with deception is that it is *deceptive!* In other words, when we are deceived, we don't know we are deceived. The closer to truth deception is, the more deceptive it is. This explains why Jesus warns, "If the light you think you have is actually darkness, how deep that darkness is!" (Mt 6:23, NLT). Moreover, we are warned, "There is a way that appears to be right, but in the end it leads to death" (Prov 16:25, NIV).

We can be sure that those 'Christians' Jesus relegates to hell in Matthew chapter seven will be taken by surprise—the surprise of their lives! It's definitely not the kind of surprise you or I want at the end of *our* lives! So for our own safety, here's the billion-dollar question we each must ask:

If many 'Christians' who call Jesus their Lord will be turned away to hell by Jesus, and if only few find the narrow path that leads to life like Jesus says, is there any possibility—even the slightest chance—that I am also one of the many who is deceived, thinking I am on the way to heaven, only to hear Jesus say, "I never knew you; depart from Me..."?

But again, how would you know if you *were* deceived, when those who are deceived don't know they are? The only one you can fully trust in this matter—the one who never lies or twists the truth—is God Himself. So before going on to chapter three, I encourage you to pause—pray and ask God to reveal any lies and distortions of truth that have sneaked into your heart. He delights in revealing the truth to a humble heart that is truly ready to let go of any and all distorted thinking. Today is your opportunity to pause and examine yourself against the words of God that are often side stepped in Christianity today.

Of course there are those religious teachers who say you should never question your salvation—that such a thing is the devil trying to undermine your faith, but God Himself encourages us to examine ourselves to see if we are in the faith.

> Examine and test and evaluate your own selves to see whether you are holding to your faith and showing the proper fruits of it. Test and prove yourselves [not Christ]. Do you not yourselves realize and know [thoroughly by an ever-increasing experience] that Jesus Christ is in you--unless you are [counterfeits] disapproved on trial and rejected? (2Cor 13:5).[2]

As you examine and question what you've thought to be true, and what your hope of salvation is based upon, compare it to God's very own words in the Bible. Ask His Holy Spirit to be your teacher.

And please don't take my words as gospel truth. Before you trust my words, be sure they are consistent with the words of God in the Bible, many of which are conveniently printed right here in this book.

I welcome you to pause now and pray. Feel free to use your own words:

"Heavenly Father, lead me not into temptation, but deliver me from evil. Reveal any lies and distortions of truth that might be in my thinking. Uncover and remove any deception such as the kind that is taking to hell so many people who call you Lord today."

1. Truth War Today. "The Frankenstein Monster Project Part 3 - The Statistics." 30 July 2010. 1 November 2011. <http://truthwartoday.blogspot.com/2010/07/frankenstein-monster-project-part-3.html>
2. See also Lam 3:40

Chapter 3

WHO GETS INTO HEAVEN?

So let's start with a key question. Why exactly, do you expect God will let you into heaven? Really and seriously, what gives you that hope or confidence? Pause and take the time to answer this key question before we go on. I know it's hard to actually stop reading to do this, but if you do, the next bit will come alive for you even more! So here's the question again; why do you expect God will let you into heaven?

Are you ready with your answer?

Is it because you believe that Jesus is God's Son who died as a sacrifice for your sins? Surely those calling Him 'Lord' in Matthew 7 will have believed this too, yet Jesus will send them off to destruction.

Is your hope based on the fact that you are baptized? Surely many of those hell bound people in Matthew 7 were also baptized if they were calling Jesus their Lord and ministering for the church!

Do you rely on the fact that you prayed a prayer inviting Jesus to be your Savior and Lord? As we'll see just below, those in Matthew 7 are also speaking to Him calling Him, "Lord, Lord," yet they will go to hell.

Some people think they'll go to heaven because they are Catholic.

Others think they'll get in because they are Protestants or Orthodox. Others expect their acts of kindness and service will make the difference. Still others hope their hours of prayer or their pilgrimage or their many confessions will help earn their way in. Then there are those who say it's only by faith in Jesus that we are saved and that good deeds don't count. Finally, there are those who say, "I'm not a bad person. I'm not perfect, but my good definitely outweighs my bad! And besides, God is a loving God. He knows I'm only human so He'll forgive me for my shortcomings and let me in."

But what does *Jesus* say? Who does *HE* say will get into heaven? The answer is simple. You will find it in verse twenty-one below, but be sure to read it in its context!

Matthew 7

13Enter through the narrow gate; for wide is the gate and spacious and broad is the way that leads a way to destruction, and many are those who are entering through it.

14But the gate is narrow (contracted by pressure) and the way is straitened and compressed that leads away to life, and few are those who find it.

15Beware of false prophets, who come to you dressed as sheep, but inside they are devouring wolves.

16You will fully recognize them by their fruits. Do people pick grapes from thorns, or figs from thistles?

17Even so, every healthy (sound) tree bears good fruit [worthy of admiration], but the sickly (decaying, worthless) tree bears bad (worthless) fruit.

18A good (healthy) tree cannot bear bad (worthless) fruit, nor can a bad (diseased) tree bear excellent fruit [worthy of admiration].

19Every tree that does not bear good fruit is cut down and cast into the fire.

20Therefore, you will fully know them by their fruits.

21Not everyone who says to Me, Lord, Lord, will enter the kingdom of heaven, but he who does the will of My Father Who is in heaven.

22Many will say to Me on that day, Lord, Lord, have we not prophesied in Your name and driven out demons in Your name and done many mighty works in Your name?

23And then I will say to them openly (publicly), I never knew you; depart from Me, you who act wickedly [disregarding My commands].

24So everyone who hears these words of Mine and acts upon them [obeying them] will be like a sensible (prudent, practical, wise) man who built his house upon the rock.

25And the rain fell and the floods came and the winds blew and beat against that house; yet it did not fall, because it had been founded on the rock.

26And everyone who hears these words of Mine and does not do them will be like a stupid (foolish) man who built his house upon the sand.

27And the rain fell and the floods came and the winds blew and beat against that house, and it fell--and great and complete was the fall of it.

28When Jesus had finished these sayings [the Sermon on the

Mount], the crowds were astonished and overwhelmed with bewildered wonder at His teaching,

29For He was teaching as One Who had [and was] authority, and not as [did] the scribes.

(Mt 7:13-29, emphasis mine)

So who gets into heaven?

Jesus says, "Not everyone who says to Me, Lord, Lord, will enter the kingdom of heaven, but <u>he who **does** the will of My Father Who is in heaven.</u>"

Who gets in? "He who **does** the will of My Father."

Who gets in? In four simple words, 'Those who obey God.'

Who? In two words, 'The repentant.'

It's simple. Those who love and trust Jesus enough to actually *obey* Him as Lord, get into heaven. Merely *calling* Him "Lord" doesn't cut it.

And did you notice the context of our key verse? Jesus is talking about the wide road that leads to destruction and the narrow road that leads to life which few people find. He warns us to beware of religious men who appear legitimate yet lead us to destruction using deceptive teaching. He tells us how to distinguish such a person from a true Christian leader. And finally, He finishes by contrasting a person who obeys Jesus, with a person who doesn't. The one who *doesn't* obey, comes to great ruin. The one who *does* obey, flourishes even when great storms come!

By now you've guessed it. Disobedience is at the heart of the false faith that is deceiving so many people who call themselves Christians. Let's have a closer look.

Chapter 4

WHAT IS THE GREAT DECEPTION?

M any who are totally convinced that they are Christians and hoping to get into heaven, will die one day and face the most terrible wake-up call ever, when Jesus says to them, "I never knew you; depart from Me" (Mt 7:23).

How can we become so deceived? And what is this great deception, this false faith, this false Gospel that is so tasty, that throngs of people are swallowing it?

In its basic form, this deception is a Christianity that frequently eliminates the need to turn from sin (repentance) to be saved. Furthermore, this deception often requires submission to man's religious traditions instead of God's will, and this submission is often confused as repentance, even when those traditions are contrary to God's words!

Repentance is where a person changes his *mind* for the better, and heartily amends his *ways*, turning to God with abhorrence of his past sins (Luke 13:3). Any gospel that does not require true repentance, is a great lie. This lie has many appealing faces, but each one is deceptively made to be believable through the use of partial truths, spun from the Bible. Often a mix of man-made ideas and tradition is added to further the deception. Many who are deceived don't even know they are disobeying God because they assume their religious teachers have told them the biblical truth, when instead they've been given man-made tradition that is contrary to God's words.

This happens in Catholic and Protestant and Orthodox circles alike, and it isn't anything new. Religious teachers were adding and subtracting from God's Word back in Jesus' day and they were severely rebuked by Him for doing so. The additions and subtractions are different today, but what is common to each version of this deceptive faith, is *a willingness to live in disobedience to God while still expecting to get into heaven.*

You may be surprised at some of the common forms this deception takes today, and you will certainly recognize them as we shine the light of biblical truth upon them to expose them.

Shall we begin?

Chapter 5

WHY SHOULD I LET YOU INTO HEAVEN?

Suppose you were to die today and you arrived before God your Judge. And suppose He was to ask you, "Why should I let you into heaven?" What would you say? The following is a list of common answers. Jump to the ones that seem most reasonable to you and explore the good, the bad and the surprising.

"Why should I let you into heaven?"

"Why should I
let you into heaven?"

Because I believe in Jesus. I believe He
died for my sins. I'm saved by faith.

It's good that you believe Jesus is God's Son who died as a sacrifice for your sins! But surely those calling Him 'Lord' in Matthew 7 will have believed this too, yet Jesus will send them off to destruction. What went so very wrong?

It's simple. They believed the history about Jesus dying on the cross, but they never actually believed the man Himself enough to follow and obey Him. They *called* Him "Lord," but did not *submit* to Him as Lord.

They had historical and intellectual belief but not *saving* belief. The difference is clear. Saving belief involves *repentance* and *obedience*. With historical and intellectual belief, you only know *about* God. With saving belief, you *know* God. The one merely gives lip service. The other obeys God. One believes *in* God. The other *believes* God. One leads to hell, the other to heaven. In God's words,

> We can be sure that we know Him[God] <u>if we obey His commandments</u>. If someone claims, "I know God," but doesn't obey God's commandments, that person is a liar and is not living in the truth. But <u>those who obey God's word</u> truly show how completely they love Him. That is how we know we are living in Him. Those who say they live in God should live their lives as Jesus did.
>
> (1John 2:3-6, emphasis mine)

That passage offers the ABC's and 1-2-3's of the most basic truth throughout the Bible—if we know and love God, we'll obey Him. By the way, did you notice the reference for this passage is made up of 1-2-3? It's the easiest reference in the Bible to remember, and in today's world, perhaps the most important!

Yes, you may say you *believe* in Jesus and that you are saved by faith, (and it's true that we are saved by faith according to Romans 5:1 and many other passages), but correctly understanding that little word *believe* makes all the difference. Even the demons believe in God, and they shudder (James 2:19). Their belief is not saving belief! We must not only believe *in* Him—we must *believe* Him and repent![1] I might say that I believe you can carry me across a tight rope from one building to another to escape a fire, but if I die in the fire refusing to be carried, my belief was mere lip service. My actions revealed the truth—I didn't believe.

The kind of belief or faith that saves our soul, is the kind that results in our obedience, but far too often, the most popular verse in the Bible, John 3:16, is understood as if it refers to historical and intellectual belief. The results are very convenient at first, allowing an unrepentant worldly lifestyle as a Christian, but of course the end result on judgment day will be shocking and devastating.

The Amplified Bible version helps us to understand the true meaning of John 3:16 by supplying several words for the word *believe* as per the original language. Read it again for the first time!

"For God so greatly loved and dearly prized the world that He [even] gave up His only begotten (unique) Son, so that whoever <u>believes in (trusts in, clings to, relies on)</u> Him shall not perish (come to destruction, be lost) but have eternal (everlasting) life" (John 3:16, emphasis mine).

Then, in the same chapter further on, it's clear that the word *believe* is effectively synonymous with the word *obey* when talking about salvation. It says, "…anyone who <u>believes</u> in God's Son has eternal life. Anyone who doesn't <u>obey</u> the Son will never experience eternal life but remains under God's angry judgment" (John 3:36, emphasis mine). So *saving* belief and disobedience are opposites with two very different destinations.

There is no room in these verses for believing *and* living an unrepentant lifestyle of disobedience at the same time. Either we believe and live a repentant lifestyle of obedience and have eternal life, or we disbelieve and live a lifestyle of disobedience and go to eternal hell.

Does your belief in Jesus include trusting in, clinging to and relying on Him in a lifestyle of obedience like the word *belief* actually means? Does your belief drive you to search out *His* words in the Bible to discover *His* will for yourself, or are you assuming your religious teachers have got it all right? Does your belief in Jesus result in obeying *Him*? Is your lifestyle patterned after Jesus' sermon on the mount? Is He really your Lord, or are you like so many others, being deceived by simply calling Him "Lord," while doing your own thing or your church's thing?

The only kind of belief or faith that saves our soul, is the kind that results in obeying God. This is one of the most basic and important truths in Scripture and it is revealed in the Bible hundreds of times, yet it is all but snuffed out in many 'Christian' circles. Appendix A offers a convenient but surprising gathering of Bible passages to show this truth. Here are just two verses from that list:

"He[Jesus] became the Author and Source of eternal salvation to all those who give heed and obey Him" (Hebrews 5:9, emphasis mine). Did you notice who gets saved according to this verse?

"So also faith, if it does not have works (deeds and actions of obedience to back it up), by itself is destitute of power (inoperative, dead)" (James 2:17).

So we see, 'belief in Jesus' or 'faith in Jesus' is only good for salvation if it is the kind of belief that prompts obedience!

Does this mean we *earn* or *merit* our salvation by our works or our obedience? Definitely not! Our salvation cannot possibly be earned by our works. On the contrary, we are saved by faith in what *Christ* did to merit our salvation. We are completely dependent on Christ's sacrificial death. Without it, there could be no salvation—no covering of our sins by perfect blood. However, our works of obedience are the crucial indication that our faith is actually in *Christ*, and not in ourselves.

Without works of obedience to Christ, our behavior proves we don't actually have our faith in Christ at all.

If we say that we believe in Jesus but we don't obey Him, we are just like those calling Jesus "Lord" in Matthew 7, whom He will send to destruction. In our deception, we can fool ourselves, but we don't fool God.

1. Mcintyre, Patrick. "The Graham Formula -- Part 2 of 7." Documentary. 1 Jan. 2008. YouTube. 18 October 2011.

"Why should I
let you into heaven?"

**Because I prayed the prayer of salvation,
inviting Jesus into my heart.**

M any people have been taught to 'accept Jesus' by saying a prayer. They've been told, "Just say this prayer and you'll be saved!"

You may have mouthed the best prayer in the world, but if you haven't lived it out, that prayer did you more harm than good, because it left you with the idea you were saved when you weren't!

Prayers, in and of themselves, don't save us. Turning from sin because of faith in Jesus is what saves us. This is called repentance. Remember what Jesus says in Matthew 7? Only those who *do the will of the Father* get into heaven. Nowhere in the whole Bible do you see Jesus or anyone else leading someone in a 'prayer of salvation'. Of course, many people have been saved at the time they prayed such a prayer, but only because they had a repentant heart. Without that, there is no salvation, regardless of what prayer is said.

Moreover, there simply isn't *any* onetime event or action that a person can do to guarantee his salvation, any more than a wedding guarantees a marriage. What is vowed and celebrated at a wedding must be lived out over time if it is to have any value. In the same way, a prayer of genuine repentance is fantastic, but if you turn from your repentance and go back to living like it never happened, you have chosen to call Jesus your Lord when in fact He isn't.

Salvation occurs at the distinct point in time that a person first genuinely repents and trusts Jesus; however, true saving repentance is a lifelong *lifestyle* of turning from sin and following Jesus because of faith in Him. Repenting isn't merely something you do once to be saved. Someone might ask, "Have you repented?" but the real question is, "Are you living in repentance?"

A 'prayer of salvation' is not repentance. At best, such a prayer can *verbalize* true repentance. Dangerously, there are many people who think of themselves as having repented because they said 'the prayer', even though they are not living a life bent on obeying God. Their life shows they haven't repented, even though they prayed 'the prayer'.

It's great to remember the special day you came to Christ—that day the Holy Spirit convicted you of sin and you came to hate the sin you once loved, and to love the righteousness you once hated[1], but to rest your confidence of salvation on that day in the past while living in disobedience is self-deception. And if there never *was* a day that God convicted you of sin, bringing you to hate the sin you once loved, and to love the righteousness you once hated, then you were never saved in the first place.

All this explains why in the following Scripture, Jesus speaks of *dwelling* with Him and *abiding* with Him. These are terms of an *ongoing* relationship, not a *onetime* event. In the following two passages, Jesus repeats this message of remaining united with Him *sixteen* times! In contrast, the alternative has to do with fire. Jesus says,

> <u>Dwell in Me</u>, and I will <u>dwell in you</u>. [<u>Live in Me</u>, and I will <u>live in you</u>.] Just as no branch can bear fruit of itself without <u>abiding</u> in (being vitally <u>united</u> to) the vine, neither can you bear fruit unless you <u>abide in Me</u>. I am the Vine; you are the branches. Whoever <u>lives</u> in Me and I in him bears much (abundant) fruit. However, apart from Me [cut off from vital <u>union</u> with Me] you can do nothing. If a person does not <u>dwell in Me</u>, he is thrown out like a [broken-off] branch, and withers; such branches are gathered up and <u>thrown into the fire</u>, and they are burned.
> (John 15:4-6, emphasis mine)

Jesus gives a great summary a few verses later that also emphasizes an *ongoing* relationship, not a *one-time-covers-all-no-matter-what* salvation event. "If you <u>keep</u> My commandments [if you <u>continue to obey</u> My instructions], you will <u>abide in</u> My love and <u>live on</u> in it, <u>just as I have obeyed My Father's commandments</u> and <u>live on</u> in His love" (John 15:10, emphasis mine).

On another occasion, Jesus was asked, "What shall I do to inherit everlasting life?" Jesus didn't offer any onetime prayer of salvation nor any other onetime religious task as the key to the door of heaven. Instead, His answer involved living out a *personal relationship*. "Love the Lord your God with all your heart and with all your soul and with all your strength and with all your mind; and your neighbor as yourself" (See Luke 10:25-28). Again, it's not a *onetime* solution, but rather a *lifetime* solution.

Even the phrase *born again* that Jesus uses, implies the beginning of a new life, which has *duration*. It is not simply an event in the past to depend upon for salvation while we go on living like the world.

I remember a dear friend who came to me quite distressed. She said, "Years ago I prayed the prayer that the evangelist told us to pray. He said if we prayed it, we'd be saved. But if I were to die today, I don't think I'd go to heaven."

Unfortunately, there are many, many people who have said a 'prayer of salvation' though they have never repented. Then, after saying the prayer, an evangelist has told them that they were saved, when in reality they were not. And making matters worse, the evangelist has often told them that they can never lose their salvation. By combining these two proclamations, the evangelist has given them the most dangerous false assurance possible. He has given them the stick of dynamite ("You're saved") *and* the fuse ("You'll always be saved") for their eternal destruction. Now the people not only think they're saved when they aren't, but they think they're saved for good! Their sense of eternal danger has practically been eliminated, and they happily call themselves Christians, even though they are not saved at all! Thankfully my friend smelled a rat and was brave enough to question what she had been taught.

It's primarily the job of the evangelist to tell people *how* to be saved, not to tell them that they *are* saved. As the great evangelist D.L. Moody taught, that second job is the job of the Holy Spirit. Moody would urge an immediate decision and encourage a person to open his mouth to cry out, "God be merciful to me, a sinner!" but Moody said, "...never tell a man he is converted. Never tell him he is saved. Let the Holy Spirit reveal that to him…"[2]

What we *can* do is tell people *how* they can know they are saved, as revealed, for example, in 1John 2:3-6 and 1John 5. These verses teach us to examine the evidence; "We can be sure that we know Him[God] <u>if we obey His commandments</u>" (1John 2:3). As Paul Washer says, "Do you have a new relationship with sin? If not, then you don't have a new relationship with God."[3]

It is interesting how people are often urged, "Ask Jesus into your heart," as if this too is a method of salvation. Sometimes Revelation 3:19-20 is quoted to support this; however, this passage is written to lukewarm believers, not to unsaved people. And when it encourages us to open the door of our life to Jesus, we are told to do so through—you guessed it—*repentance*, not by a mere prayer asking Jesus into our hearts. Paul Washer says, "The greatest heresy in the American evangelical and protestant church is that if you pray and ask Jesus to come into your heart, He will definitely come in. You will not find that in any place in Scripture."[4]

Repentance is the part that so often and readily gets missed because it requires humility to submit to a will that is higher than our own. It requires a willingness to turn from our sin and follow the way of Jesus. Only a *pretend* Jesus forgives the unrepentant, tolerates sin, doesn't mind other gods, and lets almost everyone into heaven whether they behave like the world or not, as long as they've said a prayer of salvation at some point in their life! This Jesus is far less concerned with repentance, but then again, he's unable to save us.

Have you ever been told to write the date of your salvation into your Bible so that whenever you doubt your salvation, you can look it up and tell the devil you're saved? Let me remind you; that date inked into your Bible, doesn't save you. Living a life of repentance with faith in Christ is what saves you. There may actually be a very good reason why you doubt your salvation, and ignoring that doubt because of a date written in your Bible, could be disastrous.

It's much better to examine yourself when doubts and guilt come. See more about this in Chapter 11, but any guilt you may feel is either true guilt that God is convicting you of, or false guilt and condemnation that the enemy is putting on you. Do you want to know the difference? God's conviction is specific. He pinpoints things in our lives that can be resolved with specific repentance. In contrast, guilt from Satan, the accuser, is like a nebulous dark cloud with nothing specific to resolve. If it's God saying something, repent and obey Him and enjoy the resulting freedom! If Satan is the cause of your grief, remind him you are saved and victorious by the blood of Jesus. Then send him packing in Jesus name!

To recap, are you living a repentant lifestyle? Are you actually doing the will of the Father in faith that Jesus has saved you? Is this where your hope rests? Or is your confidence of salvation merely based on prayers you have said in the past and on assurances you have heard from well-meaning Christians?

1. Washer, Paul. "Shocking Message." Sermon on Heart Cry Films. 2002. YouTube. 28 October 2011.
2. Whitesell, Faris Daniel. "D.L. Moody-The Practical Personal Worker." Krow Tracts. Post date unknown. 20 Oct. 2011. <www.krowtracts.com/articles/moody.html>
3. Washer, Paul. "I'm Not Ashamed of the Scandal." Lane Chaplin. 12 June 2008. YouTube. 28 October 2011.
4. Washer, Paul. "Shocking Message." Sermon on Heart Cry Films. 2002. YouTube. 28 October 2011.

"Why should I
let you into heaven?"

Because I was saved years ago
and I can't lose my salvation.

For many years after becoming a Christian, I was convinced my salvation was guaranteed no matter what I did. Of course this was very much a relief, especially in those periods when I chose to disobey the Lord! I had heard people teach this kind of eternal security and it seemed plausible, especially when they would quote Hebrews 13:5NKJV where God says, "I will never leave you nor forsake you." It was all the more plausible when they would quote Romans 8:38-39 which indicates that nothing in all creation will be able to separate us from the love of God which is in Christ Jesus our Lord.

In fact, this appealing teaching stayed plausible in my mind for many years until I began to see verse after verse in the Bible showing that it is clearly possible to walk away from the Lord and our salvation if we choose to. I began to record the biblical references and soon I had pages and pages of Scripture that left my jaw on the floor.

Later, I learned my wife had simultaneously been discovering the same surprising truth that I was, and she too had been gathering a list of biblical references! All this Scripture is conveniently available for you in Appendix C. In a moment, I'll share with you just a few of those passages, but first this!

Apostasy

Let's be clear. There are many who have been called Christians, who never did repent and have since appeared to backslide. Those people were never saved in the first place, and can therefore be referred to as false converts, however here we are not speaking of false converts who were never saved. Here we are speaking instead of those who *did* know Christ. The English term for abandoning our faith in rebellion is *apostasy*. Apostasy is the consequence of a deliberate choice to depart from or turn from God after experiencing real relationship with Christ. If we do this, we are abandoning the eternal security and salvation and blessings God promises to those who follow Him.

This doesn't happen quickly or accidentally. Usually it is a process of many decisions to disobey God over a period of time, until a person's faith is finally cooked, much like the proverbial frog in a slowly heated pot of water. Our Heavenly Father is incredibly patient and loving with His wayward children, calling them back again and again, but in the end, we still have the freedom to choose to follow Him or not to follow Him. Sadly, over time, enough choices to disobey God can leave us distanced and cold toward Him and very vulnerable to a foolish decision to walk away from Him as His voice becomes harder and harder to hear.

We live in an age when the teaching of apostasy has been often abandoned. This has given all the more room for the clever deception of many who feel secure in their faith while still living in sin. They feel confident of their salvation due to some salvation event in their past, and they are convinced they will remain saved no matter how they live.

Let's see what God says. Is it true that a Christian cannot abandon his salvation? Here are just a few of the many revealing passages in the Bible:

> For <u>if, after they have escaped the pollutions of the world through [the full, personal] knowledge of our Lord and Savior Jesus Christ, they again become entangled in them and are overcome, their last condition is worse [for them] than the first.</u> For never to have obtained a [full, personal] knowledge of the way of righteousness would have been better for them than, having obtained [such knowledge], <u>to turn back</u> from the holy commandment which was [verbally] delivered to them.
>
> (2Pet 2:20-21, emphasis mine)

> For it is impossible [to restore and bring again to repentance] those who have been once for all enlightened, who have consciously tasted the heavenly gift and have become sharers of

the Holy Spirit, and have felt how good the Word of God is and the mighty powers of the age and world to come, <u>if they then deviate from the faith and turn away from their allegiance--[it is impossible] to bring them back to repentance</u>, for (because, while, as long as) they nail upon the cross the Son of God afresh [as far as they are concerned] and are holding [Him] up to contempt and shame and public disgrace.

(Heb 6:4-6, emphasis mine)

<u>If we endure</u>, we shall also reign with Him. <u>If we deny and disown and reject Him, He will also deny and disown and reject us.</u>

(2Tim 2:12, emphasis mine)

If you seek to be justified and declared righteous and to be given a right standing with God through the Law, you are brought to nothing and so <u>separated (severed) from Christ. You have fallen away from grace</u> (from God's gracious favor and unmerited blessing).

(Gal 5:4, emphasis mine)

As mentioned, Appendix C provides many other passages in the Bible showing that true Christians can later turn from God to their own destruction. If you have been walking in sin thinking you will be saved, and today you are hearing God's conviction to repent, please do so now while you can still hear His call!

True Eternal Security

False eternal security guarantees a person is saved on the basis of a salvation event in his past, no matter how he lives. In contrast, here are passages that speak of *true eternal security*—the kind which is enjoyed by those who adhere to, trust in and rely on Jesus. These people may know with absolute confidence, they are saved.

"I write this to you who believe in (adhere to, trust in, and rely on) the name of the Son of God [in the peculiar services and blessings conferred by Him on men], so that you may know [with settled and absolute knowledge] that you [already] have life, yes, eternal life" (1Jn 5:13, emphasis mine).

"We can be sure that we know Him[God] if we obey His commandments" (1John 2:3).

These verses and their contexts describe the rock solid eternal security and assurance of salvation we have when we truly follow Christ, loving Him and obeying Him. Put that together with the promise of God at the beginning of 2Timothy 2:12 quoted just above, and we know beyond any doubt that, "If we endure, we shall also reign with Him."

True eternal security for the repentant person comes from knowing that God is faithful to keep His promises, but to top it off, God has also given true believers His Holy Spirit as a seal and a security deposit to assure us of salvation (2Cor 1:22)[1]. "The one who keeps God's commands lives in him, and he in them. And this is how we know that he lives in us: We know it by the Spirit he gave us" (1Jn 3:24, NIV, emphasis mine).

This however, does not eliminate *endurance* as the condition on which we retain our salvation as we see here; "Then note and appreciate the gracious kindness and the severity of God: severity toward those who have fallen, but God's gracious kindness to you--provided you continue in His grace and abide in His kindness; otherwise you too will be cut off (pruned away)" (Rom 11:22, emphasis mine).

Once Saved, Always Saved

So what about those passages that people quote to prove they can't lose their salvation? How do they fit with all of this?

It's not difficult. First, keep in mind that what God promises to the faithful, is often opposite to what He promises to the unfaithful. His promises are often conditional upon our obedience. In the case of Hebrews 13:5, His promise to never leave or forsake us, is a promise to those who walk with Him, not a promise to those who don't.

As for Romans 8:38-39, it holds true that for as long as we choose to walk with God, nothing is powerful enough to overcome God's power and separate us from His love. His love will always be there for us if we choose to walk in it. However, there is one thing that is absent from the list of things that can never separate us from God's love—OUR SIN!! These verses misapplied have given much comfort to the Christian who continues in his sin.

There is another passage sometimes used to prove 'once saved always saved'. It is John 10:27-28 where Jesus speaks about His sheep, saying that no one is able to snatch them out of His hand. This is true of His sheep. However it is not true of His non-sheep. He defines His sheep right in this very passage to be those who follow Him. Living a life of disobedience is choosing not to be His sheep. Living a life of disobedience is choosing to get out of His hand, a dangerous option that Scripture often warns sharply against as it warns us to persevere and endure in order to be saved.

As we read above in 2Pet 2:20-21, turning from your repentance, leaves you worse off than you were before you first repented. I wouldn't have believed this myself if it wasn't so abundantly and repeatedly clear in Scripture, but these truths are supported over and over by the irrefutable pages and pages of Scripture you'll find in Appendix C.

No doubt, many of those 'Christians' whom Jesus will relegate to hell, will wind up there because they had a false assurance of salvation, a belief that once they were saved, they would always be saved, no matter how they lived.

---

1. See also 2Tim 3:5, 1Cor 4:20, 1Jn 4:13, Acts 1:8, Acts 5:32

"Why should I
let you into heaven?"

Because I try to be a good person.

B eing good is good! Giving to the poor, praying faithfully, volunteering, going to church, helping the widow, healing the sick, fasting, even preaching—it's all good. The problem is, it just isn't good enough. No matter how hard we try, we can't achieve God's perfect standard of righteousness because we are still sinners. We have all fallen *short* of God's glorious perfection (Rom 3:23).

Have you ever lied? That makes you a liar. Ever stolen anything? That makes you a thief. Ever looked at a woman with lust? Jesus says that makes you an adulterer (Mt 5:28). That's just three of the Ten Commandments. And how about this; have you ever *not* done the things that you *should* do?[1]

None of us comes close to God's righteous perfect standard. Compared to how good others are, you might score yourself a 90 out of 100, but when comparing yourself to God's standard, you need to compare yourself to infinity, not to 100! Of course 90 compared to infinity, is nothing!

The only man who is infinitely perfect is Jesus. He's willing to cover us in His infinite righteousness if we trust Him to do so, but trying to get into heaven on the merits of our *own* goodness is futile. That amounts to faith in ourselves rather than faith in Jesus. A sinner is as capable of saving himself, as a dead battery is capable of boosting itself!

Now let's be clear. As crucial as it is to obey God, our obedience is not a payment to merit or earn our salvation. Obedience is simply evidence of our faith in Jesus—faith that He gives us the *free gift* of Salvation at the time we choose to follow Him. All the *paying* has already been done by Him when He shed His perfect and infinitely costly blood to pay for our sin. Though we obey God with a great love for Him, we still have *nothing* perfect or pure with which to cover our sin, except the blood of Jesus. This is why Paul says,

For it is by <u>free</u> grace (God's <u>unmerited</u> favor) that you are saved (delivered from judgment and made partakers of Christ's salvation) through [your] faith. And this [salvation] is not of yourselves [of your own doing, it came <u>not through your own striving</u>], but it is the <u>gift</u> of God. Not because of works [not the fulfillment of the Law's demands], lest any man should boast. [It is not the result of what anyone can possibly do, so no one can pride himself in it or take glory to himself.]

(Eph 2:8-9, emphasis mine)

In fact, when we get to thinking that we can somehow accomplish something good in payment for our salvation, be it more prayers or more kindness or more sacrifice, God brings us back to reality with Isaiah's words. "We are all like one who is unclean, all our so-called righteous acts are like a menstrual rag in your sight. We all wither like a leaf; our sins carry us away like the wind" (Is 64:6, NET).

Doing good is good. Obeying God is good. But there is only one who *is* good—God Himself. The rest of us need His mercy and grace! Jesus said, "There is no one [essentially and perfectly morally] good--except God alone" (Mark 10:18).

Do you recall those poor people in Matthew 7 who will wind up in hell even though they'd been calling Jesus their Lord? Did you notice their list of good deeds? They will tell Jesus, "Have we not prophesied in Your name and driven out demons in Your name and done many mighty works in Your name?" (Mt 7:22). Wow! If good deeds could earn our salvation, they would be in! Unfortunately, they'll be out!

Their hope is that their good deeds will outweigh their bad, regardless of their lack of obedience. If only those people would have instead trusted Jesus enough to obey Him. Then *His* righteousness would be credited to their account. Instead, their faith is in their *own* good works, thinking *they* can somehow attain to God's standard themselves.

In the same way, there are many today trying to be good enough to please God, hoping their good works will pacify God, causing Him to disregard their disobedience. They do many good deeds and jump through man-made religious hoops, following this church tradition and that, hoping God is pleased with all their many prayers and fasts and sacrifices and self punishments, etcetera, etcetera, when in affect, what they are trying to do is pay for their own sin. They are trying to add to or improve on what Jesus finished at the cross. God is not impressed—and why would He be? Here's what He says to those trying to earn a righteous standing by obeying *His* Law, let alone by obeying *man's* religious laws.

> If you seek to be justified and declared righteous and to be given a right standing with God through the Law, you are brought to nothing and so <u>separated (severed) from Christ</u>. You have <u>fallen away</u> from grace (from God's gracious favor and unmerited blessing).
>
> (Gal 5:4, emphasis mine)[2]

It's clear. Trying to be good enough to attain our *own* righteous standing before God, ensures we will fall short! But to repent and obey Jesus, is to trust in *His* goodness and *His* perfection to cover us. *He* insures our salvation.

By the way, have you noticed the apparent contradiction here? On one hand the Bible teaches we are saved by faith and not by our own works or striving (Eph 2:8-9), yet on the other hand, we are told to repent and obey Jesus to be saved. Such obedience requires work. Hard work! It requires striving! In fact both Hebrews 4:11 and Luke 13:24 tell us to 'strive' diligently to be saved.

"Strive to enter by the narrow door [force yourselves through it], for many, I tell you, will try to enter and will not be able" (Luke 13:24).

Isn't this a contradiction? Actually, there isn't a contradiction here, but the appearance of one has caused much confusion, with some people saying we are saved by works of obedience, and others saying we are saved by faith. While it's true that we can't save ourselves by good works, many in the Christian church today are so afraid of the word *works* (not recognizing that there are different kinds of works described in Scripture according to 1Thess. 1:3; Eph. 2:10; Acts 26:20) that they have denied the reality that faith and repentance both require evidence (or fruit) to prove their existence (Acts 26:20; Jas. 2:17-20).[3]

The confusion is easily cleared up when we understand what our striving accomplishes, and what it *does not* accomplish. Simply put, the striving required of us, is the difficult work of obeying Jesus—following Him, becoming like Him by the power of the Holy Spirit. These works of obedience do *not* accomplish our own righteousness to satisfy God's standard of perfection. They can't even *begin* to accomplish that. What they *do* accomplish for our salvation is much more humble than that. These works of obedience indicate that our faith is in *Jesus*, and that we are totally reliant on the righteousness *He* can cover us with. By obeying Jesus and not someone else, we are indicating that we believe it is only through *Him* that we can have a righteous standing that meets God's standard of perfection.

With our works, we could never merit or earn a righteous standing before God. It is *Christ's* work, *Christ's* sacrifice, *Christ's* perfect shed blood that pays for our sin and justifies us before God. This is God's gift to us. However, our way of saying 'yes' to that gift, is by having faith enough to repent and obey Jesus. That involves the working or striving that Hebrews 4:11 and Luke 13:24 speak of. Without these works of obedience, we prove we have no faith in Christ.

Therefore, it is accurate to say, we are saved by the kind of faith that is demonstrated by good works, not by faith that has no practical evidence, for such a faith would be an empty profession. That would be the kind of faith that results in Jesus saying, "I never knew you. Depart from me."

Take faith or works away, and you are lost. You need both. The absence of one, invalidates the other. But having noted the important role of works, let's never twist this to mean that we could ever earn or deserve our salvation by being good! A thousand times, never!

1. Comfort, Ray. "Hell's Best Kept Secret." Sermon. 2006. livingwaters.com. 18 October 2011.
2. See also Galatians 3
3. Krow, Don. "Repent and Be Converted." Krow Tracts. Date posted unknown. 20 Oct. 2011.

"Why should I
let you into heaven?"

Because I confessed my sins.

Confession is good, but let's look again at the people in Matthew 7:21 who call Jesus their Lord. According to them, they prophesied in Jesus' name and drove out demons in His name. Chances are they also confessed their sins and did a lot of other good stuff not listed in this verse, yet Jesus rejects them on judgment day. So how is it possible that someone who confesses his sins can wind up in hell?

Simple. It is entirely possible to admit we are wrong without any intent to change! Put another way, it is entirely possible to confess our sins without repenting. Repenting means to turn from our sin to follow the way of Jesus. Trust and repentance that leads to a lifestyle of obedience is the key.

It is one thing for a true Christian who is running in the right direction, to confess his sin after tripping and falling. It is another thing for an unrepentant false Christian to confess his sin while running the wrong direction as he normally does, with no plan of repentance.

God already knows the bad we've done. He doesn't benefit from being given the list again. His *real* interest is in whether or not we are *turning* from our sins to follow Him. It is within *this* context of humble repentance that confessing our sins takes on a helpful role. Confession in the context of a repentant life helps us to keep short accounts with God, but confession without repentance has no saving power whatsoever.

This is obvious when we remember we are speaking of a person-to-person relationship here. What if someone repeatedly hurt you and confessed, then hurt you and confessed, then hurt you and confessed, on and on without any evidence that he intended to change his behavior? He might be soothing his conscience by confessing, but if he has no intention of changing, he might as well stop his hypocritical act of confession! In the case of our relationship with God, He sees our heart and knows the truth when we confess.

Some people rely heavily on 1John 1:9 to assure themselves they are saved. It reads, "If we <u>confess</u> our sins, He is faithful and just to forgive us our sins and to cleanse us from all unrighteousness" (NKJV, emphasis mine).

This verse assures us of God's patient fatherly love that is always willing to forgive a repentant heart. But if read in its context, this verse gives no assurance of salvation to an unrepentant sinner simply because he has verbally confessed his sin. On the contrary—just three verses earlier, John says, "If we say that we have fellowship with Him, and walk in darkness, we lie and do not practice the truth" (John 1:6, NKJV).

Some people also rely heavily on Romans 10:9 to assure themselves they are saved even if they aren't walking in submission to Jesus. It reads; "If you acknowledge and confess with your lips that Jesus is Lord and in your heart believe (adhere to, trust in, and rely on the truth) that God raised Him from the dead, you will be saved."

I purposely quoted this from the Amplified Bible as a reminder of what that little word *believe* actually means. It means to *adhere to*, trust in, and rely on the truth. *Adhering* to Christ involves obeying His teachings. This verse does not provide an easy back door into heaven without the need of true repentance—a change of mind and a change of ways is required. That is the definition of repentance.

I'm afraid for the multitudes of people who will die in the false hope that they will get into heaven because they confessed their sins and confessed Christ and 'believed' in Him, calling Him "Lord," but they never turned from their sin to follow Him. They will hear from Christ, "I never knew you; depart from me, you who act wickedly [disregarding My commands]" (Mt 7:23)

"Why should I
let you into heaven?"

Because I'm a Catholic, or
…I'm a Protestant, or
…I'm Orthodox, or
…I'm a Christian.

Whether we are Catholic, Protestant, Orthodox, or something else, we often think of ourselves as being part of the "correct" religious group. It bolsters our hope and confidence; however, the Bible is clear—each of us will be judged as an *individual*. We won't stand before our Judge in groups or denominations. "But I tell you that everyone will have to give account on the day of judgment for every empty word they have spoken. For by your words you will be acquitted, and by your words you will be condemned" (Mt 12:36-37, NIV).[1]

Regardless of our religious association, we will each be held accountable as an *individual* to one and the same standard—the standard Jesus revealed in Matthew 7:21. You remember it… "He who does the will of my Father Who is in heaven," will enter the kingdom of heaven.

Since that is the case, it is *absolutely crucial* to know what the will of the Father really *is*—not merely the pastor's will, not merely the priest's will, not merely the bishop's will, not merely the pope's will, but *God's* will. That's why it's so important for us to read God's message in the Bible for ourselves, to hear His voice *directly, individually* and *personally,* today. If we wait till judgment day to hear His voice directly and personally, it will be too late to make any course corrections. By then, we would have followed the crowd and made all the same mistakes as those around us—the same fatal mistakes made by those many in Matthew 7 who call Jesus their Lord and minister in Jesus name before being sent to hell.

Perhaps you've been taking comfort in knowing you are part of a particular church or religious affiliation or tradition, hoping this might save you. By now you can see how dangerous that assumption is. In each of the traditions, there is the potential for many members, even at very high levels, to *call* Jesus their Lord while not *following* Him as Lord. Instead they could be following men, and traditions of men, or even their own lusts for power and riches and pleasure.

It is entirely likely that there are people in *your* religious group who are deceived to some degree or another, but even if that were not the case—even if you are part of an excellent God-honoring group, no one enters heaven on the basis of his religious membership. It is always on the basis of our *individual* standing before God.

It may seem surprising, but Jesus wasn't a Catholic or a Protestant or a Greek Orthodox; in fact, he wasn't even called a Christian! This is because all four of these terms were invented well after Jesus had returned to heaven! The name *Christian* for example, was first used in Antioch well after the great persecution and scattering of the early church according to Acts 11:26. The names *Catholic* and *Protestant* and *Greek Orthodox* and the many other denominational names are much more recent terms not mentioned anywhere in the Bible. We would be wise not to identify more strongly with our church name, than with the name of *Jesus!* The point is to know our God *Yahweh* and to follow *Him* and to love *Him* and to worship *Him* through His Son Jesus. The point isn't to glory in our religious tradition or to depend on it for salvation.

By the way, do you think Abraham, Moses, King David, and John the Baptist got into heaven? Of course! But were they members of your specific religious denomination or tradition? What about the thief on the cross who was saved before he died? Was he a member of your specific religious tradition? Actually, he missed the confessional and baptism and church membership altogether. He didn't even get to take his first communion—but what he didn't miss, is the one thing we all need to do—he turned from sin, putting his faith in Jesus (Luke 23:39-43).[2]

The evidence of his repentance is clear; After mocking Jesus together with the others, he was convicted of his sin and he stopped mocking. He turned to Jesus, believing that Jesus was the Messiah, and he asked for salvation. His humble repentance and faith was immediately visible by his change in behavior and by his verbal request. After his change, he even tried to help his fellow criminal to see the truth about his sin and about Jesus. Jesus gave him salvation, even though he had no church membership, no baptism, no nothing—except faith in Jesus that led to repentance!

We can agree then, that being a member of your religious tradition or my religious tradition is no guarantee of salvation, nor is it the prerequisite for salvation. In the end, the question still is, "Did we do the will of the Father Who is in heaven?"

Let's look at what John the Baptist said to people who based their hope on membership in the 'correct religious group'. These guys thought they were in good shape because they were from the group of Abraham, but John said,

> You brood of vipers! Who warned you to flee from the coming wrath? Produce fruit in keeping with <u>repentance</u>. And do not think you can say to yourselves, 'We have Abraham as our father.' I tell you that out of these stones God can raise up children for Abraham. The ax is already at the root of the trees, and every tree that does not produce good fruit will be cut down and thrown into the fire.
>
> (Mt 3:7-10, NIV, emphasis mine)

It's clear. Without repentance, without turning from sin to follow God's will, membership in the world's best church won't save us.

Adding and Subtracting from the Bible

Now then, whatever your specific Christian tradition or denomination, there is a common and dangerous pitfall to avoid. It is the tendency over time in every tradition, to add or subtract from what God has said in the Bible. This can happen unintentionally over time, much like a photocopy of a photocopy of a photocopy gets further and further from the original, adding more and more distortion with each generation. This happens in Christian traditions unless the people are very intentional about letting the Bible trump tradition whenever the two conflict.

Adding and subtracting from the Bible distorts our understanding of *the Father's will.* That's tremendously dangerous, because *the Father's will* is the very standard we will be measured by at the end of our lives! No one wants to follow a map to heaven that has been fiddled with or falsified, only to have Jesus say, "I never knew you; depart from Me" (Mt 7:23). So let's be sure we are following *God's* map, not man's!

God warns, "Do not add to what I command you, and do not subtract from it, but keep the commands of the LORD your God that I give you" (Deut 4:2, NIV). Any religious leader who thinks he is above this commandment of God is a very dangerous person to follow.

In previous chapters, we have already seen how repentance is something often *subtracted* in Christian traditions, but let's look now at some teachings that man has *added.* We know that church leaders must have the authority to establish rules in order to keep order and harmony. The problem comes when their rules and traditions contradict God's Word, *especially when these man-made traditions become additional expectations for salvation, or when these traditions offer other ways of salvation.* Titus 1:9-14 sharply rebukes those who follow man-made laws that contradict God's Word.

Listed below are some popular traditions and teachings that you won't find in the Bible. Some of these are helpful traditions, some are relatively inconsequential, but others are contrary to God's Word and are thus, very deceptive.

Traditions of Men

Added Tradition or Doctrine Not Found in the Bible	Date Added (A.D.)	Biblical Evaluation
Once saved, always saved regardless of lifestyle	57[3]	Already in Paul's day he needed to clarify for the Roman Christians that their inheritance of God's grace did not give them a license to sin, but rather to go on sinning would lead back to death (Rom 6:15-23).
Infant baptism	3rd Century[4]	We have no examples of infant baptism in the Bible. The closest we have is certain 'households' being baptized but we don't know the ages of those involved and we can't assume they included infants. There is also no teaching in the Bible to encourage infant baptism. On the contrary, the Bible indicates that Baptism is meant to be an outward or public proclamation of an inner personal choice a person has made to follow Jesus—the kind of choice no infant is capable of making. Baptism has no saving power, but rather, it is the celebration of someone who has already been saved (Acts 8:37-38, 10:47-48, 19:5, Rom 6:3-5). Jesus Himself was baptized as an adult, in keeping with other examples in Scripture (Mt 3:13-15). Another example is when the eunuch wanted Philip to baptize him. The eunuch was only allowed to be baptized if he was prepared to obey Jesus. "And Philip said, If you believe with all your heart [if you have a conviction, full of joyful trust, that Jesus is the Messiah and accept Him as the Author of your salvation in the kingdom of God, giving Him your obedience, then] you may [be baptized.]" (Acts 8:37-38, emphasis mine). Today many people who are not following Jesus, hope they'll be saved because of their infant baptism. Many others put their hope of

		salvation in their adult baptism even though they are not following Jesus. Both are hoping for a salvation that does not require repentance. Both will be shocked and disappointed if they don't repent.
Praying to Mary and the saints	300[5] (although not common till much later)[6]	"This, then, is how you should pray: "'Our Father in heaven, hallowed be your name" (Mt 6:9, NIV). As we see here, when Jesus teaches us how to pray he teaches us to address our Father in heaven. This is consistent with His personal example. Nowhere in all of Scripture is there teaching or an example that encourages addressing Mary or any other human in prayer. Scripture is clear about the One who has authority to be our Mediator and exactly what qualifies Him as such; "But He[Christ] holds His priesthood unchangeably, because He lives on forever. Therefore He is able also to save to the uttermost (completely, perfectly, finally, and for all time and eternity) those who come to God through Him, since He is always living to make petition to God and intercede with Him and intervene for them. [Here is] the High Priest [perfectly adapted] to our needs, as was fitting--holy, blameless, unstained by sin, separated from sinners, and exalted higher than the heavens" (Heb 7:24-26). The qualifications listed above are not met by any woman or man other than Jesus. Clearly, we have bold and confident access to God through none other than Jesus Christ. "In Whom, because of our faith in Him, we dare to have the boldness (courage and confidence) of free access (an unreserved approach to God with freedom and without fear)" (Eph 3:12). The bold and confident access God promises us through Jesus Himself, is doubted and questioned when we feel we have a better hope of being heard by Mary than by God through Jesus. A greater confidence in prayers to Mary comes from hope that she will have a greater pull with Jesus since she is His mother, but nothing in Scripture even suggests she or

the saints in heaven can hear our prayers.

If she *could* hear our prayers and observe our bowing to her, she would follow in the example of angels and apostles. What did they do when people bowed down to them in reverence? Here's Peter's example:

"As Peter entered the house, Cornelius met him and fell at his feet in reverence. But Peter made him get up. 'Stand up,' he said, 'I am only a man myself'" (Acts 10:25-26, NIV).

Even angels refuse to receive the kind of reverence often given to Mary:

"I, John, am the one who heard and saw these things. And when I had heard and seen them, I fell down to worship at the feet of the angel who had been showing them to me. But he said to me, 'Don't do that! I am a fellow servant with you and with your fellow prophets and with all who keep the words of this scroll. Worship God!' (Rev 22:8-9, NIV, emphasis mine).

On the flip side, Isaiah corrects people in the habit of praying to the dead saying, "Why consult the dead on behalf of the living? (Is 8:19, NIV).

Crossing yourself with the sign of the cross	310[7]	Encourages remembrance of the triune God and a key biblical event. Unfortunately, it can also amount to a fetish, a superstition or a good luck charm.
A date selected to celebrate Christ's resurrection	325[8]	Encourages remembrance and celebration of a key biblical event.
Dec 25th selected to celebrate Christ's birth	4th Century[9]	Encourages remembrance and celebration of a key biblical event.
Stained glass windows	4th Century[10]	A relatively inconsequential tradition today, though it was once a key teaching tool helping illiterate people to learn the chronological story of God.
Wearing the cross on clothes or jewelry	5th Century[11]	Encourages remembrance of a key biblical event. Unfortunately, some also use it as a fetish or a good luck charm.
Steeples on churches	Approx. 600[12]	A relatively inconsequential tradition, although bell towers can be helpful to call people to worship.

Bible divided into chapters and verses	1227 and 1551[13,14]	Greatly assists in Bible study.
Purgatory—a state of temporary punishment for the purification of a person who is bound for heaven, though not pure enough to go to heaven directly	1439[15]	The concept of purgatory is found nowhere in the Bible. The Bible refers to only two realities for believers. We are either still at home in our body and absent from the Lord, or we are absent from our body and present with the Lord. The latter refers to a pleasing experience, not to one of punishment. This is clear in the following verse: "We are confident, yet, well <u>pleased</u> rather to be absent from the body and to be present with the Lord" (2Cor 5:8, NKJV, emphasis mine). For believers, punishment for sin has been fully taken care of by Jesus in a way that can't be improved on. It is only the blood of Jesus that cleanses us from all unrighteousness. That leaves exactly zero cleansing left for us to take care of in purgatory. Our own suffering for a million years couldn't improve on or assist the finished work of Jesus who said on the cross, "It is finished!" (John 19:30). "Therefore, there is now no condemnation for those who are in Christ Jesus" (Rom 8:1, NIV).[16] The idea that someone can pray and pay your way through into heaven after you die is foreign and opposite to Scripture which teaches, "It is appointed for [all] men once to die, and after that the [certain] judgment" (Heb 9:27). As for the glorification or transformation that believers look forward to, the Bible speaks nothing about the process involving temporary punishment. Rather it is a work of Jesus' power, "Who, by the power that enables him to bring everything under his control, will transform our lowly bodies so that they will be like his glorious body" (Phil 3:21, NIV).[17]
The Apocrypha proclaimed to be on par with the 66 books of the Bible at the Roman Catholic Council of Trent	1546[18]	The Apocrypha is made up of seven books and two additions to Esther and Daniel that were never regarded as sacred Scripture by the Jews who were the keepers of God's Word.[19] These books do not meet the canonical standard that qualified all other books in the Bible.[20]

		These books include doctrines in variance with the Bible. For example, Tobit 12:9 counters 1John 1:7. It indicates that alms deliver from death and purge away sins, but the Bible speaks of the blood of the lamb—the blood of Jesus, being necessary to do this.[21] The New Testament never refers even once to the Apocrypha books[22], whereas the New Testament refers to the books of the Old Testament hundreds of times. The Latin Vulgate Bible, comes primarily from Jerome's translation of the Scriptures into Latin. Jerome was determined not to include the Apocrypha since it was not in the Hebrew Scriptures, however others added it to the Vulgate later. It is therefore rather ironic that about one thousand years after Jerome did his translation, the Council of Trent would 1) canonize the Latin Vulgate to include the Apocrypha, and 2) at the same council, declare Jerome's own views about the Apocrypha to be anathema. In effect, they accepted Jerome's translation as their standard Bible, but if he had been alive at the time, they would have had to excommunicate their main translator for his opinion regarding the Apocrypha! Instead, he's named as a saint! Go figure.
The immaculate conception of Mary—Mary did not know sin.	1864[23]	The Bible teaches that <u>ALL</u> men are sinners, with one obvious exception—Jesus. "Therefore, as sin came into the world through one man, and death as the result of sin, so death spread to <u>all</u> men, <u>no one</u> being able to stop it or to escape its power because <u>all</u> men sinned" (Rom 5:12, emphasis mine). "For <u>all</u> have sinned and fall short of the Glory of God" (Rom 3:23, NKJV, emphasis mine). The one exception is Jesus, and this exception is plainly spelled out throughout Scripture in many places because it is such a notable and unusual exception. No other exception is mentioned. And surely such a notable thing would have been mentioned in the Gospel accounts if it were true of someone else.

		But indeed the opposite is revealed in the gospel account, for if Mary did not know sin, why did she call God her Savior? "And Mary said, My soul magnifies and extols the Lord, And my spirit rejoices in God my Savior" (Lk 1:46-47). This invented doctrine helps to position someone other than Jesus to receive worship and adoration and prayer that only Jesus deserves. It draws people to depend on Mary who can't save them, in place of Jesus who can.
The pope, called *Holy Father*, is infallible and has supreme power of jurisdiction over the whole Christian church, and anyone who questions this man's authority is anathema (meaning cursed, hated and excommunicated). --Vatican I[24]	1870[25]	Jesus says, "Do not call anyone [in the church] on earth father, for you have one Father, Who is in heaven" (Mt 23:9, emphasis mine). There is only one Holy Father and He is God, not a mere man. Jesus sharply rebukes the Pharisees for accepting such titles and commands us not to title a church leader Father—let alone Holy Father. Given that Peter the apostle is said to be the first in a succession of popes, you would think he might at least have been the head of the Jerusalem church, but he wasn't. According to Galatians 2, Acts 12:17 and Acts 15:13, the head of the Jerusalem church was James, not Peter.[26] And though Peter was clearly an important leader in that church, he received severe and public correction from Paul on a theological matter (Gal 2:11-14). This is not at all in keeping with any pope status we have invented today. The Bible knows nothing of a universal church leader other than Christ, the Head of the Church. The title 'universal bishop' was used for the first time in history, by Boniface III in 607A.D. after the wicked emperor Phocas offered Boniface the title in order to spite the bishop of Constantinople.[27] Therefore, there is no so-called unbroken 'apostolic succession' or 'papal succession' from Peter onward. Truer to history, the papacy has been bought and sold and bartered. It was invented and reinvented. There were as many as three who all called themselves popes at the same time, fighting for power. Then there was Alexander VI who bought the papacy. The papacy was a big battle for power. To help establish that power, the papacy got centered in Rome.

The Pope wanted to affirm and magnify his power and so he created the idea of papal succession and started filling in the gaps going backward, however, there were periods of time when there was no bishop in Rome at all...304 to 308, 638 to 640, 1085 to 1086, 1241 to 1243, 1269 to 1271, 1292 to 1294, 1314 to 1316, 1415 to 1417. Papal succession is not only unbiblical but unhistorical. There's no succession here, and certainly no divine succession. [28]

Peter is said by some, to be the first pope, and the following passage is sometimes quoted as support for this:

"And I tell you, you are Peter [the Greek here is Petros--a large piece of rock], and on this rock [the Greek here is petra--a huge rock like Gibraltar] I will build My church, and the gates of Hades (the powers of the infernal region) shall not overpower it [or be strong to its detriment or hold out against it]" (Mt 16:18, emphasis mine).

In this passage, the 'rock' that Christ is building His church on is understood by some to be Peter, however, if you look at this verse, Peter is only the large piece of rock(Petros), in keeping with his name. The huge rock(petra), like Gibraltar which Jesus is building His church on, is the truth concerning Jesus which Peter had just proclaimed—the truth that Jesus is the Christ, the Son of the living God! On this truth—on this great rock, Jesus is building His church.

The relatively recent proclamation in 1870 of the pope's supreme authority (noted here on the side), effectively cuts off and curses every one in every other Christian tradition outside his own 'one true church', calling all others anathema(to be hated and excommunicated). This is now considered doctrine by the Roman Catholic tradition in spite of the fact that close to half of the Roman cardinal-bishops voted against it! [29]

In sharp contrast to this partisan spirit, Scripture rebukes people who identify themselves as belonging to one man or another.

		"For when one says, I belong to Paul, and another, I belong to Apollos, are you not [proving yourselves] ordinary (unchanged) men? What then is Apollos? What is Paul?" (1Cor 3:4-5).
		In the same way that Paul questions, "What then is Apollos? What is Paul?" we must also ask, "What then is the pope?" In the case of Paul and Apollos, when people said, "I belong to you," Paul rebuked them. However in the case of the pope, instead of rebuking this partisan spirit, the pope nurtures it and demands it, saying that anyone who doesn't comply to his headship is to be cursed, hated, and excommunicated! It's hard to imagine this could be true, but it's right in the Vatican statements, and it's nurtured with lavish pomp and ceremony wherever he goes.
		One of the most dangerous of the invented doctrines common today is the one that has effectively authorized this elected man to create new doctrines, even when those doctrines are contrary to Scripture.
The assumption of Mary	1950[30]	Mary is greatly blessed. This we know from Luke 1:46-49. Whether or not she was assumed into heaven like Enoch was, the Bible doesn't say. Only recently has this become dogma in some circles.
"For after being assumed into heaven, she [Mary] has not put aside this saving function, but by her manifold intercession, she continues to win the gifts of eternal salvation for us."[31]	1965[35]	"I [Jesus] am the Way and the Truth and the Life; no one comes to the Father except by (through) Me" (John 14:6). This excludes salvation through Mary.
		"And there is salvation in and through no one else, for there is no other name under heaven given among men by and in which we must be saved" (Acts 4:12).
		When Jesus went to heaven, the Father sent us His counselor, the Holy Spirit, to help us--not Mary:
		"And I [Jesus] will ask the Father, and he will give you another advocate to help you and be with you forever—the Spirit of truth. The world cannot accept him, because it neither sees him nor knows him. But you know him, for he lives with you and will be in you" (John 14:16-17, NIV).

Mary is the gate of heaven, Mediatrix of all graces, Mirror of Perfection, Mother of the Church, Mother of Mercy, Pillar of faith, Seat of Wisdom[32,33]	1996	In the words of a former Polish cardinal, "Victory when it comes will be a victory through Mary."[36] In contrast, the Bible says, "But thanks be to God, Who gives us the victory [making us conquerors] through our Lord Jesus Christ" (1Cor 15:57, emphasis mine). While Mary played a very important role in fulfilling the virgin birth of Jesus, she would never supplant or replace Christ's role as Savior. She is not our Mediator nor is she the gate of heaven. These are descriptions of Jesus and Him alone.
"Mary is the way which leads to Christ."[34]	1997	"So Jesus said again, I assure you, most solemnly I tell you, that I Myself am the Door for the sheep. All others who came [as such] before Me are thieves and robbers, but the [true] sheep did not listen to and obey them. I am the Door; anyone who enters in through Me will be saved" (John 10:7-9, emphasis mine). The term Mediatrix refers to Mary as a Mediator in the process of our salvation. However, God's Word says; "For there [is only] one God, and [only] one Mediator between God and men, the Man Christ Jesus" (1Tim 2:5).

Obeying religious traditions of men rather than God's Word is not a new problem. Jesus sharply rebuked the *highest* religious leaders of his day for this very thing here in the Gospel of Mark:

"'These people honor me with their lips, but their hearts are far from me. They worship me in vain; their teachings are merely human rules.' You have let go of the commands of God and are holding on to human traditions. And he continued, "You have a fine way of setting aside the commands of God in order to observe your own traditions! ...Thus you nullify the word of God by your tradition that you have handed down. And you do many things like that."

(Mark 7:6-9, 13, NIV, emphasis mine)[37]

Regarding leaders who mislead with traditions and teachings that are contrary to His word, Jesus warns us as disciples, "Leave them; they are blind guides. If the blind lead the blind, both will fall into a pit" (Mt 15:14, NIV).

To underline just how dangerous false teachers are, Jesus indicates here that they lead people to hell! "Woe to you, teachers of the law and Pharisees, you hypocrites! You travel over land and sea to win a single convert, and when you have succeeded, you make them twice as much a child of hell as you are" (Mt 23:15, NIV). Clearly, whom we choose to follow is a very, very, important decision!

Some people might ask, "But won't God let me off the hook if a wrong teacher has misled me? Isn't it the fault of the teacher?" It is partly the fault of the teacher that you were misled, and he will be accountable for his part, but he is not accountable for your part—choosing to follow him when God warned you not to follow false teachers and false prophets.

Remember what happened to the people who followed Korah and other false leaders in Moses' day? They got swallowed alive by the same ground that swallowed their false leaders (Num 16:33). Instead of just blindly following a religious leader, God expects us to be like the Bereans who scrutinized Paul's teachings according to Scripture before they followed him.[38]

Unfortunately, there are many dear people today called Christians who are less like the Bereans and more like those described in 2Corinthians 11:20. They blindly follow on even when deceived, controlled, and taken advantage of by their religious leaders; "For you endure it if a man assumes control of your souls and makes slaves of you, or devours [your substance, spends your money] and preys upon you, or deceives and takes advantage of you, or is arrogant and puts on airs, or strikes you in the face." Submitting to spiritual abuse endangers our souls, but using biblical discretion to wisely choose our spiritual leaders, protects us from being deceived and misled.

Still, there are millions of people today who are convinced by their religious leaders that the Bible is too difficult to understand—that only religious leaders can be trusted to interpret it. This false idea is one of the most powerful lies used by false 'Christian' leaders to maintain their control over those who are in the dark and subservient to their unbiblical doctrines. In contrast, we ought to be people who can say to the Father, "I have hidden your word in my heart that I might not sin against you" (Psalm 119:11, NIV).

False 'Christian' leaders are infamous for making the Bible say whatever they want it to by twisting and pulling things out of context just as Satan used bits and pieces of God's words to deceive Eve. It's the oldest trick in the book, and it works like a charm against people who haven't hidden God's Word in their hearts. The inventing of deceptive doctrines will continue until Jesus returns, but those who are willing to, can learn what is true by studying the Bible for themselves, and taking it at face value. When it comes to reading the Bible, may God help us to believe what we read, and to stop simply reading into it what we've always believed.

In summary, membership in the world's best church won't save us, but turning from sin to follow God with faith in Jesus will. And if we are *doing the will of the Father Who is in heaven*, then certainly we would agree with Him that His son Jesus is the Way, the Truth, and the Life and no man comes to the Father except through Him (John 14:6).

This then excludes trying to get to the Father through our denomination, or through Mary, or through our pastors, or through the saints, or through the pope or through priests or through Billy Graham or through anyone else. Jesus alone is our Savior and our Mediator! (1Tim 2:5).

Religious leaders can be helpful, but they are not our Savior or our Mediator. Mary is greatly blessed, but she is not our Savior or our Mediator. The 'saints' might have been saintly, but they are not our Savior or our Mediator. Denominations can be helpful but they are not our Savior or our Mediator. On the contrary, we are wise to remember that 'fathers' here on earth can actually give instruction that is very different from the will of the Father in Heaven!

God reminds us to hide His Word in our hearts so that we might not sin against Him (Psalm 119:11). That's the surest way to know the difference between His will and any traditions of men that might be contrary. Let's not confuse repentance as submission to man's traditions when those traditions are contrary to God's will. Rather, let's be sure we are doing the will of the *right* father, the Father *Who is in heaven*, so we will never hear the words from Jesus, "I never knew you; depart from Me, you who act wickedly [disregarding My commands]."[39]

1. See also Jer 17:10, Prov 16:2 and 1Cor 4:5

2. See also Mt 27:44, Mark 15:32

3. Anonymous notes preceding "The Epistle of Paul the Apostle to the Romans". The Open Bible; New Living Translation, Nashville: Thomas Nelson. 1998. pp. 1483.

4. Infant baptism." *Wikipedia, The Free Encyclopedia*. Wikimedia Foundation, Inc. 14 Oct 2011. Web. 18 Oct. 2011.

5. MacDonald, David and Kirsten. "Mary in the Early Church and Today." Catholic Bridge. Post date unknown. 19 Oct 2011.

6. Van Enns, Arlyn. Noted Dec 22, 2011.

7. Testa, Stephen. "Is Romanism in the Bible." Christian Independent Missionary Association. Post date unknown. 19 Oct. 2011.

8. "Easter." *Wikipedia, The Free Encyclopedia*. Wikimedia Foundation, Inc. 14 Oct 2011. Web. 19 Oct. 2011.

9. "Christmas." *Wikipedia, The Free Encyclopedia*. Wikimedia Foundation, Inc. 23 Sept 2011. Web. 19 Oct. 2011.

10. "Stained Glass." *Wikipedia, The Free Encyclopedia*. Wikimedia Foundation, Inc. 11 Oct 2011. Web. 19 Oct. 2011.

11. "Pectoral Cross." *Wikipedia, The Free Encyclopedia*. Wikimedia Foundation, Inc. 20 Aug 2011. Web. 19 Oct. 2011.

12. "Steeple (architecture)." *Wikipedia, The Free Encyclopedia*. Wikimedia Foundation, Inc. 28 June 2011. Web. 19 Oct. 2011.

13. "1000AD-1600AD". *Christian Resource Library*. NicheNets. 24 Sept. 2010. Web. 19 Oct. 2011.

14. Vlach, Mike. "How We Got Our Bible." NTS Library Online. Aug 1999. 19 Oct. 2011.

15. Testa, Stephen. "Is Romanism in the Bible." Christian Independent Missionary Association. Post date unknown. 19 Oct. 2011.

16. See also 1John 1:7-9, 1John 2:1-2, and John 19:30.

17. See also 1Jn 3:2.

18. Testa, Stephen. "Is Romanism in the Bible." Christian Independent Missionary Association. Post date unknown. 19 Oct. 2011.

19. Vlach, Mike. "How We Got Our Bible." NTS Library Online. Aug 1999. 19 Oct. 2011.

20. Vlach, Mike. "How We Got Our Bible." NTS Library Online. Aug 1999. 19 Oct. 2011.

21. Mizzi, Paul. "The Apocrypha." Truth For Today. 2011. 19 Oct 2011. <http://www.tecmalta.org/tft108.htm>

22. Vlach, Mike. "How We Got Our Bible." NTS Library Online. Aug 1999. 19 Oct. 2011.

23. Testa, Stephen. "Is Romanism in the Bible." Christian Independent Missionary Association. Post date unknown. 19 Oct. 2011.

24. "First Vatican Council Session 4 Chapter 3." EWTN Global Catholic Network. Post date unknown. 19 Oct. 2011. <www.ewtn.com/library/councils/v1.htm>

25. Testa, Stephen. "Is Romanism in the Bible." Christian Independent Missionary Association. Post date unknown. 19 Oct. 2011.

26. MacArthur, John. "The Pope and the Papacy." Grace to You. 1 May 2005. 19 Oct 2011.

27. Mizzi, Paul. "The Petrine Heresy." Truth For Today. 2011. 19 Oct 2011. <www.tecmalta.org/tft309.htm>

28. MacArthur, John. "The Pope and the Papacy." Grace to You. 1 May 2005. 19 Oct 2011.

29. Van Enns, Arlyn. Noted Dec 22, 2011.

30. Testa, Stephen. "Is Romanism in the Bible." Christian Independent Missionary Association. Post date unknown. 19 Oct. 2011.

31. Most, William. "Mary, Mediatrix of All Graces." Quote from The Second Vatican Council (Lumen gentium ## 61-62). EWTN Global Catholic Network. Post date unknown. 19 Oct. 2011. <www.ewtn.com/faith/teachings/marya4.htm>

32. John Paul II, *John Paul II's Book of Mary* (Huntington: Our Sunday Visitor, 1996), Table of contents.

33. "General Audiences: Teaching Of Pope John Paul II On The Blessed Virgin Mary." EWTN Global Catholic Network. Post date unknown. 19 Oct. 2011. <http://www.ewtn.com/library/mary/jp2bvm70.htm>

34. Pope John Paul II. "Devotion To Mary Is Based On Jesus' Will." EWTN Global Catholic Network. Post date unknown. 19 Oct. 2011. <www.ewtn.com/library/papaldoc/jp2bvm50.htm>

35. "Assumption of Mary." *Wikipedia, The Free Encyclopedia*. Wikimedia Foundation, Inc. 15 Oct 2011. Web. 19 Oct. 2011.

36. "Text of John Paul II's Last Will and Testament." Polish American Journal. 17 March 2000. 19 Oct. 2011. <http://www.polamjournal.com/Library/Papal_Polonica/Last_Will/last_will.html>

37. See also Mt 15:9 and Col 2:8.

38. Acts 17:10-11

39. Mt 7:23

"Why should I
let you into heaven?"

Because I believe God is a loving
God, and Jesus died for the
whole world, including me.

We might think that all or most of mankind will wind up in heaven. After all, didn't Jesus love the *whole world* and give His life as a sacrifice for the *whole world?* Let's consider the most popular verse in the Bible to see if this is so:

"For God so greatly loved and dearly prized the world that He [even] gave up His only begotten (unique) Son, so that whoever believes in (trusts in, clings to, relies on) Him shall not perish (come to destruction, be lost) but have eternal (everlasting) life" (John 3:16, AMP, emphasis mine).

Yes, we see here that God greatly loves the world, but what else do we see here? First, we see there are two eternal destinies to choose from. One involves destruction. The other involves eternal life. Secondly, we see there is a condition for eternal life—it is *believing in, trusting in, clinging to, and relying on* Jesus. Apparently, not everyone in the world goes to heaven.

It's true—Jesus *did* die for the whole world; however, most of the world is choosing to reject His free gift.

Have you ever given your love to someone who didn't love you back? This can happen because people are free to choose whom they will love. We can't force another person to love us. To try, would be contrary to the very definition of love. We can love them and woo them but we can't force them to love us back.

Neither does God force us to love Him. That wouldn't be love! We can reject Him if we want to, but because He loves us, He has extended to us (yes, to the whole world), an infinitely valuable gift of salvation. The choice is ours as individuals, whether to take the gift and reciprocate the love of God or not. If we choose to reciprocate His love, we do so by trusting His son Jesus and turning from our sinful ways to follow Him in intimate relationship.

This also helps answer the old question, "How could a loving God send someone to hell?" This is an odd question when you realize that God, more than anyone, has gone to great personal expense to keep people *out* of hell. People choose hell for themselves if they wish to reject His love and costly gift of salvation.

Imagine a person is sentenced to death for murder, but out of love, the son of the judge takes the murderer's death penalty. Then the judge gives the murderer a choice, either to accept the gift of freedom, or to reject it and pay the death penalty again for himself. Foolishly, the murderer rejects the gift, but when the judge sentences him to death, he turns indignantly to the judge and says, "How could a loving judge give me the death penalty?" Obviously, the fool by his own choice, gave *himself* the death penalty, leaving the judge no other choice but to follow through with justice.

We leave the just Judge of heaven no other choice if we choose to reject Jesus and pay our death penalty ourselves. Someone must pay it, for God cannot wink at sin without become guilty Himself. "For the wages which sin pays is death, but the [bountiful] free gift of God is eternal life through (in union with) Jesus Christ our Lord" (Rom 6:23).

Although the idea of an eternal prison called hell may seem unbelievable or difficult to accept, it is interesting how much Jesus taught on the subject. Here are some verses that bring out hell's clear reality. Many others can be found in Appendix B:

"Do not be afraid of those who kill the body but cannot kill the soul. Rather, be afraid of the One who can destroy both soul and body in hell" (Mt 10:28, NIV).

"And if anyone's [name] was not found recorded in the Book of Life, he was hurled into the lake of fire" (Rev 20:15).

"Enter through the narrow gate, because the gate is wide and the way is spacious that leads to destruction, and there are many who enter through it. But the gate is narrow and the way is difficult that leads to life, and there are few who find it" (Mt 7:13, NET).

Clearly, there is a heaven and a hell, and by individual choice, many more people are on the wide road that leads to destruction. This is not God's desire for them though. He loves us all. He is "Not willing that any should perish but that all should come to repentance" (2Pet 3:9, NKJV).

"Why should I
let you into heaven?"

**Because I had a life changing
experience with God.**

God uses many fascinating ways to get our attention. Sometimes His methods are surprising and quite unusual—even heart-stopping and life changing. The talking donkey in Numbers 22 is one of the strangest events recorded in the Bible, but it was God's way of getting Balaam's attention. Even today, many people have experienced special dreams, visions, extraordinary healings, amazing miracles, even encounters with angels and demons that have been used to get their attention.

Just this week someone told me of how she didn't even believe in demons when one day, she saw a cat-man-like demon standing in her living room, looking at her with eyes that didn't blink! God allowed this encounter. It woke her up to the reality of the good and bad spirit realms, and God quickly got her attention. She took steps to discover God and has since come to follow Jesus.

On the road to Damascus, Saul (later called Paul the apostle) had a life changing experience that dropped him to the ground in a daze! A sudden light from heaven flashed around him and a voice spoke. Those with him were terrified. Paul was astonished. He was blinded for three days. When it was all done, Paul was on a completely different path of life. Until then, he had been persecuting Jesus, but from that point on, He was a follower and an ambassador for Jesus (Acts 9).

Whatever your special life changing experience was, here's the most important question; Did the experience prompt you to know and trust and obey Jesus? In other words, has your life changing experience prompted you to *"do the will of the Father Who is in heaven?"*

You may have had the most incredible one-time experience, but it won't get you into heaven if you don't choose to do the will of the Father Who is in heaven. What about those people in Matthew 7 who call Jesus their Lord, yet they are rejected and sent to hell? They too tell of experiencing miraculous things. They even claim to have *done* miraculous things in Jesus name! Still, their special experiences have no saving power in and of themselves and they will go to eternal destruction.

Some people stake their hope of salvation on a special one-time event that happened to them in the past, even though it has not resulted in them "doing the will of the Father in Heaven." But God is clear…we can't afford to rest our hope of salvation on an event in the past if we aren't living out our faith in obedience to Him. If Paul the apostle had not turned from sin to follow Jesus in faith as a lifestyle, his Damascus road event would never have saved him.

Chapter 6

WHAT IS THE WILL OF THE FATHER?

A Quick Review

> *"Not everyone who says to Me, Lord, Lord, will enter the kingdom of heaven, but <u>he who does the will of My Father Who is in heaven</u>" (Mt 7:21, AMP, emphasis mine).*

Fact 1: There is clear evidence in the Bible that many unsuspecting 'Christians' will go to hell even though they call Jesus their Lord.

Fact 2: The people who *do* get to heaven, are the ones who *do* the will of the Father Who is in heaven.

Fact 3: Today there are many powerful deceptions that keep people believing they are saved when they are not. Such people will hear the terrible words from Jesus, "I never knew you; depart from me," because they did not *do* the will of the Father Who is in heaven.

Then What *Is* the Father's will?

These simple facts leave us with an extremely important question: *If our salvation hinges on doing the will of the Father, <u>then what is the Father's</u>*

will? What do we need to *do?* The universal answer is simple and there is only one answer; His will is that we trust *and obey* His Son Jesus. God says this many times in a variety of ways so we can more fully understand it. Let's look at just five examples:

Example one: On the mount of transfiguration, God the Father spoke out of a cloud and answers our question. Referring to Jesus He said, "This is My Son, the [most dearworthy] Beloved One. <u>Be constantly listening to and obeying Him!</u>" (Mark 9:7, emphasis mine).

Example two: Here Jesus answers our question by saying,

> This is the work (service) that God asks of you: that you <u>believe</u> in the One Whom He has sent [that you cleave to, trust, rely on, and have faith in His Messenger]." "I assure you, most solemnly I tell you, he who <u>believes in Me [who adheres to, trusts in, relies on, and has faith in Me]</u> has (now possesses) eternal life.
> (John 6:29 & 47, emphasis mine)

So what is the Father's will? In a few words, the answer to our question is; *trust* and *obey* God's son Jesus—not just trust, but adhere to Him… *obey* Him.

Example three: In Luke 10:27 Jesus answers our question by affirming this statement; "You must love the Lord your God with all your heart and with all your soul and with all your strength and with all your mind; and your neighbor as yourself." Jesus explains what it means to love Him in John 14:23; "<u>If a person [really] loves Me, he will keep My word [obey My teaching]</u>; and My Father will love him, and We will come to him and make Our home (abode, special dwelling place) with him" (emphasis mine). Alternatively, "If we claim to have fellowship with him and yet walk in the darkness, we lie and do not live out the truth" (1John 1:6, NIV).

What then is the Father's will? We are to love God with our entire person and be fully submitted in obedience to His Son. That takes tremendous trust. So in a few words, the answer is again, *trust* and *obey* God's son Jesus—not just trust, but *obey* Him.

Example four: In John 3:16 Jesus says, "For God so greatly loved and dearly prized the world that He [even] gave up His only begotten (unique) Son, so that <u>whoever believes in (trusts in, clings to, relies on) Him</u> shall not perish (come to destruction, be lost) but have eternal (everlasting) life" (emphasis mine).

Obviously we must trust or believe in Jesus, but we learn more about what that means when the *opposite* of believing is described later in the same chapter.

> And he who believes in (has faith in, clings to, relies on) the Son has (now possesses) eternal life. But <u>whoever disobeys (is unbelieving</u> toward, refuses to trust in, disregards, is not subject to) the Son will never see (experience) life, but [instead] the wrath of God abides on him. [God's displeasure remains on him; His indignation hangs over him continually].
>
> (John 3:36, emphasis mine)

Clearly, if you believe, you obey. And if you don't obey, you are not believing. So in a few words, our answer is again, *trust* and *obey* God's son Jesus—not only an intellectual trust, but a trust that obeys Him. Obedience and trust can't be separated. Obedience is part of trusting, while disobedience is refusal to trust. Either a person believes and obeys, or he doesn't believe and disobeys. It's impossible to truly believe *while* living a life of disobedience.

Example five: Did you notice how Jesus summarizes His sermon on the mount? He has just warned that many who call Him "Lord" will wind up in hell. Then He clarifies God's general expectation by speaking about two kinds of people. One is saved and one is not. He says,

> So everyone who hears these words of Mine <u>and acts upon them</u>

[obeying them] will be like a sensible (prudent, practical, wise) man who built his house upon the rock. And the rain fell and the floods came and the winds blew and beat against that house; yet it did not fall, because it had been founded on the rock. And everyone who hears these words of Mine and does not do them will be like a stupid (foolish) man who built his house upon the sand. And the rain fell and the floods came and the winds blew and beat against that house, and it fell--and great and complete was the fall of it.

(Mt 7:24-27, emphasis mine)

In each of our examples, the answer is apparent—the will of the Father is that we *trust* and *obey* His son Jesus—not merely trusting the historical facts about Him, but *obeying* Him. Clearly, a person must trust Jesus enough to *obey* Jesus, if one hopes to enter heaven.

Chapter 7

THE DEVIL'S IN THE DETAILS—LITERALLY

Just Believe?

Many people today preach, *"Just believe* and you will be saved." They say we are saved by faith alone. This is true if you understand that saving belief or faith includes repentance and obedience, but in everyday use, the word *believe* does not include the ideas of repentance and obedience. As a result, repentance and obedience can easily be missed by hearers of the message, *"just believe."* People are often left thinking that intellectual agreement with historical facts about Jesus is all that is required to believe, and with that, they call themselves Christians. They go through life living in disobedience, thinking they are covered by God's grace because they've 'believed'. The devil couldn't be more pleased about their condition.

As you can see from the verses quoted in the previous chapter and in Appendix A, saving faith or belief is not simply an intellectual acknowledgement that certain facts about Jesus are true. The faith that saves us, is a *life turning faith marked by an obedience that stems from repentance.* Repentance is a turn FROM sin and a turn TO God's way. Without this turn, a person is lost. Calling Jesus "Lord" without turning to obey Him doesn't cut it. Thinking of ourselves as Christians without obeying Jesus, leads to shocking and heart-sinking words from Jesus at life's end. True faith in Jesus, is indicated by obeying Him. Any other faith in Jesus is a farce.

But Isn't God Gracious and Merciful?

Often people believe the lie that God is okay with sin since He's a gracious, loving, and merciful God. But if He *was* okay with sin, He wouldn't have gone to such pain and expense to deal with it! And what He did to deal with it only benefits the repentant, not those who choose to continue in a lifestyle of sin.

Someone might ask, "How bad could just a little tiny sin be? Like, what if I eat something I wasn't supposed to? That's not a big deal is it? God's gracious, right?"

Well, it changed the whole world when Adam and Eve committed that "little" sin, because in the end, the apparent size of the sin isn't the issue, and the devil knows it. The issue is one of pride and distrust and rebellion against God—thinking we know better than God. Any sin, even a so-called "small" sin, separates us from God and ultimately results in someone's death, either yours or Christ's.

Someone else might say, "But that was before in the Old Testament. We live in the New Testament church age now where God is much more merciful and gracious, right?" I doubt Ananias and Sapphira would agree. Both husband and wife were slain by God the day they lied about giving all the money from their house sale to the church.[1] Yes, sin leads to sickness and death even in the New Testament church age; in fact we are warned that many in the church have gotten sick and died because they took the Lord's Supper in an unrepentant state (1 Cor 11:27-31).

The fact that God has already dealt with sin by going to the cross, doesn't make our sin any less serious. On the contrary, now that we have witnessed the cross, we know even more clearly than the Old Testament saints, how serious sin is. We should then turn from it all the more. The cross makes God's grace available. It doesn't make God more tolerant of sin!

God has *always* been gracious and merciful. That is His character, and His character doesn't change (James 1:17). In fact, He's no more gracious and merciful today than He was in the Old Testament. Consider how our God Yahweh introduces Himself here in Exodus:

> The Lord passed by before him [Moses] and proclaimed: "The Lord, the Lord, the compassionate and gracious God, slow to anger, and abounding in loyal love and faithfulness, keeping loyal love for thousands, forgiving iniquity and transgression and sin. But he by no means leaves the guilty unpunished, responding to the transgression of fathers by dealing with children and children's children, to the third and fourth generation."
>
> (Exodus 34:6-7, NET)

He's the same God today. He loves us dearly, and He's exceedingly compassionate and gracious and slow to anger, but He's also a just God who cannot wink at sin.

"But," someone might say, "All my sins have been forgiven, past present and future. I've already been made righteous by the blood of Jesus—I'm covered in His blood so God can't see my sin—He sees me as cleansed, holy and righteous and He loves what He sees!"

Really? Does God *always* love what He sees when He looks at His children? Michael Brown[2] answers this with a very good question. "If the Lord always sees us as holy and righteous and always loves what He sees, why did he rebuke the believers in Laodicea, telling them that they were 'wretched, pitiful, poor, blind and naked' (Rev. 3:17)?"

Michael goes on to say, "It is because God loves us that he rebukes us (not condemns us) and it is because sin is so destructive that he calls us to turn from it. This is the goodness of God, and this is what grace does, as Paul wrote in Titus 2:11-12, "For the grace of God that brings salvation has appeared to all men. It teaches us to say 'No' to ungodliness and worldly passions, and to live self-controlled, upright and godly lives in this present age."

Michael laments, "How tragic it is today when God's people mistake the voice of His correcting love for the condemning voice of Satan, and how sad it is when they resist the purifying work of the Spirit, claiming that there's nothing to purify since God no longer sees their sins."

Perfection Required?

Does this mean we must be perfect and never sin in order to get to heaven? Not at all. If that were so, then even Abraham, Moses, King David, and all the apostles have missed the boat. Scripture acknowledges that we stumble many times (James 3:2). While God's perfect standard is our target, perfection along the way is *not* the requirement. Repentance is an issue of *direction*, not *perfection*.[3]

Let me illustrate. A golfer aims for *perfection,* which in his case is a hole in one, but if *perfection* were required to win, he would fail. Instead, he continually shoots the ball in the direction of the right hole, and given enough course corrections, the ball eventually arrives. On the other hand, shooting *away* from the hole would guarantee failure.

Life in Christ is similar. By repenting, we establish *God's perfection* as our end target. And even though *perfection* on earth is impossible, we have set course to grow in that *direction.* We continually make course corrections, aiming to become more and more like Jesus as we obey Him out of a growing love for Him. When we *do* fail, we ask for forgiveness, adjust course, and resume running in the *direction* of our patient and loving Father.[4] Therefore, the question is not, "Have I done enough to be saved?" Rather, the question is, *"Am I growing in the right direction?"*

A Life of Repentance

Essentially, we have just described what it means to live a life of repentance...a life that has turned FROM the things of the world, the flesh and the devil, and turned TO the things of God. It is not only a change of *mind,* but a change of *ways* (Mark 6:12), so the word *obey* is often used as a near substitute for the word *repent.* Here is a summary of what we turn *from* and what we turn *to.*

> For all that is in the world--the lust of the flesh [craving for sensual gratification] and the lust of the eyes [greedy longings of the mind] and the pride of life [assurance in one's own resources or in the stability of earthly things]--these do not come from the Father but are from the world [itself].
>
> (1 John 2:16)

> Now the doings (practices) of the flesh are clear (obvious): they are immorality, impurity, indecency, Idolatry, sorcery, enmity, strife, jealousy, anger (ill temper), selfishness, divisions (dissensions), party spirit (factions, sects with peculiar opinions, heresies), Envy, drunkenness, carousing, and the like. I warn you beforehand, just as I did previously, that those who do such things shall not inherit the kingdom of God. But the fruit of the [Holy] Spirit [the work which His presence within accomplishes] is love, joy (gladness), peace, patience (an even temper, forbearance), kindness, goodness (benevolence), faithfulness, gentleness (meekness, humility), self-control (self-restraint, continence). Against such things there is no law [that can bring a charge].
>
> (Gal 5:19-23)

The writer of Ephesians puts it this way. "Take no part in *and* have no fellowship with the fruitless deeds *and* enterprises of darkness, but instead [let your lives be so in contrast as to] expose *and* reprove *and* convict them. For it is a shame even to speak of *or* mention the things that [such people] practice in secret" (Eph 5:11-12). (As an aside, today we live in a world that takes pride in broadcasting and publicly parading many behaviors that used to be done in secret. Since it's shameful to mention what the disobedient do in secret, consider how much more shameful is it to entertain ourselves with such content in music, movies, TV shows, and games?)

Repentance and Obedience is Crucial for Salvation

So does our salvation depend on our repentance and obedience? Yes it does. God's grace and mercy is sufficient for the *repentant,* but His grace and mercy does not save the *unrepentant.* To use the golf analogy, we must be shooting for the right hole if we hope for God's saving grace and mercy to apply to us.

This doesn't suggest we could ever be good enough to *earn* our salvation. Not in the slightest, but rather, our repentance and obedience indicates we have a *true and real* faith in our Lord Jesus. Our obedience *earns* and *merits* no salvation, but it establishes that Jesus is truly our Lord.

It is only in the context of such a relationship, that by faith, we can expect *Jesus Christ's* perfection to cover us in order that we meet God's perfect standard. It is *Jesus Christ's* perfection alone that covers us and enables a restored relationship with God and entry into heaven. This is accomplished by the sacrifice of His perfect sinless lifeblood on our behalf. By our active faith in *Him,* we are justified, 'just as if we had never sinned!' On the other hand, faith lacking repentance and obedience is the kind of disastrous faith of those who will say, "Lord, Lord," before Jesus forsakes them to hell.

1.   Acts 5:10-11
2.   Michael Brown, "Confronting the Error of Hyper-Grace." *Charisma News*, February 18, 2013, http://www.charismanews.com/opinion/38297-confronting-the-error-of-hyper-grace
3.   Krow, Don. "Repent and Be Converted." Krow Tracts. Date posted unknown. 20 Oct. 2011. <www.krowtracts.com/books/repent_and_be_converted.pdf>
4.   Col 3:9-10, 1John 1:9, 2:6

Chapter 8

THE SAVING MESSAGE OF
JESUS AND HIS APOSTLES

The message of Jesus and His apostles was not today's popular
message that says, "Just believe and be saved," subtracting the need
for repentance and obedience while adding an unbiblical grace. Nor was
it the message that says Jesus did everything necessary for our salvation,
leaving us to do nothing. If that were true, *everyone* would be going to
heaven! Neither was their message an instruction to say a prayer, or to
try and be good enough, or to belong to the right religious tradition, or
to follow various man-made traditions.

Jesus and the apostles didn't preach these messages and neither did the
great evangelists D.L. Moody, Charles Spurgeon, John Wesley, Charles
Finney, George Whitfield, and Jonathan Edwards.[1] These men preached
about God's law to bring about a realization of sin. They warned about
God's judgment, and encouraged repentance and faith in Christ (Rom
3:20).[2] They knew that if you don't preach God's law to reveal sin and
prompt repentance, you will almost certainly get false conversions. How
true! The evidence of that is all through the church today because of the
false gospels listed above.[3,4]

The great preacher C. H. Spurgeon rebuked preachers that brushed
lightly over the uncomfortable subjects of sin and judgment and the

need for repentance. He said, "Ho, ho, sir surgeon, you are too delicate to tell the man that he is ill! You hope to heal the sick without their knowing it. You therefore flatter them; and what happens? They laugh at you; they dance upon their own graves. At last they die! Your delicacy is cruelty; your flatteries are poisons; you are a murderer. Shall we keep men in a fool's paradise? Shall we lull them into soft slumbers from which they will awake in hell?"[5]

In contrast to such flattery and the popular happy talk that is often mistaken as the preaching of the gospel, the salvation message of Jesus and His apostles was, *"Repent and believe."* In other words, the expectation of Christ and the apostles was that people *trust* plus *obey* God's son Jesus. This is exactly the same as the *will of the Father in heaven* which we looked at in chapter six. Any idea that faith is possible without obedience is foreign to their message.

In a moment, we'll look at some examples of their message, but before we do, notice this. Often in Scripture, the words *repent* and *believe* are both used to describe the human's role in salvation, because both are necessary for salvation.[6] However, at other times, only one word or the other is mentioned. This is because within the context of salvation, the meaning of one is implied in the other. Both don't have to be said every time, but both are to be understood.

This makes sense since *belief* in Jesus means to adhere to, trust in, rely on, and have faith in Him (John 6:47, AMP). You can't have that kind of belief without repenting, nor could you repent without believing. And neither can you repent (change your mind and ways) without obeying, nor could you obey without repenting. This explains why, when the Bible prescribes what is required to be saved, the word *repent* is sometimes substituted by the words *obey, heed,* and *adhere to,* while the word *believe* is often substituted by the words *faith* and *trust.*

Whatever the choice of wording, Christ and the Apostles are absolutely clear—*the first move that any sinner must make who wants reconciliation with God is repentance resulting in obedience.*[7] Scripture is full of passages calling us to repent for salvation. Many of these are conveniently quoted in Appendix A, but here are some that quickly expose any gospel of 'faith' that doesn't require repentance and obedience:

I [Jesus] tell you, No; but <u>unless you repent</u> (change your <u>mind</u> for the better and heartily amend your <u>ways</u>, with abhorrence of your past sins), you will all likewise perish and be lost eternally.

(Luke 13:3, emphasis mine)

And [Jesus] said to them, Thus it is written that the Christ (the Messiah) should suffer and on the third day rise from (among) the dead, and that <u>repentance [with a view to and as the condition of] forgiveness of sins should be preached</u> in His name to all nations, beginning from Jerusalem.

(Luke 24:46-47, emphasis mine)

But constantly and earnestly I [Paul] bore testimony both to Jews and Greeks, urging them to <u>turn in repentance</u> [that is due] to God <u>and</u> to have <u>faith</u> in our Lord Jesus Christ [that is due Him].

(Acts 20:21, emphasis mine)

He[Christ] became the Author and Source of eternal <u>salvation to all those who give heed and obey Him.</u>

(Heb 5:9, emphasis mine)

The Lord does not delay and is not tardy or slow about what He promises, according to some people's conception of slowness, but He is long-suffering (extraordinarily patient) toward you,

<u>not desiring that any should perish</u>, but that all should turn to <u>repentance</u>.

(2Peter 3:9, emphasis mine)

And Philip said, If you <u>believe</u> with all your heart [if you have a conviction, full of joyful trust, that Jesus is the Messiah and accept Him as the Author of your salvation in the kingdom of God, giving Him your <u>obedience</u>, then] you may [be baptized]. And he replied, I do believe that Jesus Christ is the Son of God.

(Acts 8:37, emphasis mine)

That is why I told you that you will die in (under the curse of) your sins; for if you do not <u>believe</u> that I am He [Whom I claim to be--if you do not <u>adhere to</u>, trust in, and rely on Me], you will die in your sins.

(John 8:24, emphasis mine)

But be doers of the Word [<u>obey</u> the message], and not merely listeners to it, betraying yourselves [into deception by reasoning contrary to the Truth].

(James 1:22, emphasis mine)

[Jesus asks] But what do you think about this? A man with two sons told the older boy, 'Son, go out and work in the vineyard today.' The son answered, 'No, I won't go,' but later he changed his mind and went anyway. Then the father told the other son, 'You go,' and he said, 'Yes, sir, I will.' But he didn't go. Which of the two <u>obeyed</u> his father? They replied, 'The first.' Then Jesus explained his meaning: "I tell you the truth, <u>corrupt tax collectors and prostitutes will get into the Kingdom of God before you do</u>. For John the Baptist came and showed you the right way to live, but you didn't believe him, while tax collectors and prostitutes did. And even when you saw this happening, you refused to believe him and repent of your sins.

(Mt 21:28-32, NLT, emphasis mine)

You believe that God is one; you do well. So do the demons believe and shudder [in terror and horror such as make a man's hair stand on end and contract the surface of his skin]! Are you willing to be shown [proof], you foolish (unproductive, spiritually deficient) fellow, that faith apart from [good] works is inactive and ineffective and worthless?

(James 2:19-20, emphasis mine)

There is no doubt. *To be merely listeners of the word and not doers of it, is to betray ourselves into deception and destruction.* Trusting *plus* obeying, is what Jesus and the apostles taught as the way of salvation. Attending church weekly and reading our Bibles to listen and listen and listen to God some more without obeying Him, is the 'Christian' way to damnation.

Salvation by Good Works?

But if our salvation is dependent on our good works of obedience as we see above, isn't this a salvation by good works and not by faith? No, not at all. A salvation by good works, supposes that our good deeds can in someway *earn* or *merit* forgiveness and a righteous standing before God. That is not what Jesus teaches. Our works of repentance and obedience don't *merit* or *earn* our salvation, but rather, they demonstrate that Jesus is our Lord in whom we have faith.

Our works of obedience do not in any way pay for our sins or cover our sins or meet God's righteous standard. Without Christ's work on the cross, all the obedience in the world wouldn't save us! It is the finished work of Christ on the cross—His sinless blood sacrificed for us, which makes salvation a possibility. If we wish to say yes to this possibility, we do so by obeying Him, in *faith* that *His* sacrificial work will then save us. *Our faith is not in our lifestyle of obedience. Rather, our lifestyle of obedience shows whom our faith is in. Jesus!*

> For it is by free grace (God's unmerited favor) that you are saved (delivered from judgment and made partakers of Christ's salvation) through [your] faith. And this [salvation] is not of yourselves [of your own doing, it came not through your own striving], but it is the gift of God; Not because of works [not the fulfillment of the Law's demands], lest any man should boast. [It is not the result of what anyone can possibly do, so no one can pride himself in it or take glory to himself.]
>
> (Eph 2:8-9)

Clearly, our works of repentance can't save us by contributing to any righteousness of our own. All our so-called righteous acts are like a menstrual rag in God's sight (Is 64:6, NET). Having said that, we can't be saved without our works of repentance and obedience, nor can we be saved without Christ's work on the cross. Both are required. His work is required to atone for our sin, and our work is required as evidence of our faith in Him as our Lord, much the same as faithfulness by definition, follows genuine marital vows.[8]

Judged by Our Works?

Speaking of works, did you know that God will actually judge us according to our works? This is because our works are a perfect indication of whom we trusted, and what we believed, and what our rewards should be, good or bad. From our behavior, God knows our belief! This may be surprising for some who have assumed they wouldn't be judged by their works, but here is the truth of the matter straight from God's Word:

"Behold, I [Jesus] am coming soon, and I shall bring My wages and rewards with Me, to repay and <u>render to each one just what his own actions and his own work merit</u>" (Rev 22:12, emphasis mine).

So we see that Christ and the apostles considered obedience a crucial ingredient of saving faith. Not only does our obedience indicate whom our faith is in, but it indicates to God what our final reward shall be.

1. Mcintyre, Patrick. "The Graham Formula -- Part 2 of 7." Documentary. 1 Jan. 2008. YouTube. 18 October 2011.
2. Comfort, Ray. "Hell's Best Kept Secret." Sermon. 2006. livingwaters.com. 18 October 2011.
3. Keith Mason, "Are you a True Christian or a False Convert?" *San Diego Evangelism*, February 18, 2009, <http://sandiegoevangelism.wordpress.com/2009/02/>
4. Whitesell, Faris Daniel. "D.L. Moody-The Practical Personal Worker." Krow Tracts. Post date unknown. 20 Oct. 2011. <www.krowtracts.com/articles/moody.html>
5. Spurgeon, Charles Haddon. "Coming Judgment of the Secrets of Men." 2001. The Spurgeon Archive. 1 November 2011. <http://www.spurgeon.org/sermons/1849.htm>
6. Mark 1:15, Acts 19:4 are examples.
7. Krow, Don. "Repent and Be Converted." Krow Tracts. Date posted unknown. 20 Oct. 2011. <www.krowtracts.com/books/repent_and_be_converted.pdf>
8. See section 4 of chapter 5 for more on this.

Chapter 9

ENDURANCE TO THE END

For those who hope to enter heaven, there is one more extremely important aspect to know about the *will of the Father in heaven*. It's simple, but not easy. It is this:

God requires that we endure to the end. A lifestyle of repentance and faith in Jesus is exactly that—a style of *life*. We must endure to the end of our lives, or we will be rejected by God.

"If we endure, we shall also reign with Him. <u>If we deny and disown and reject Him, He will also deny and disown and reject us</u>" (2Tim 2:12, emphasis mine).

"But he who <u>endures</u> to the end will be saved" (Mt 24:13, emphasis mine).

Back to the golf analogy, you may have led the pack for most of the game, but if at the last hole, you turn and go off shooting backwards down the course, you lose.

As mentioned earlier, abandoning Christ or abandoning our repentance, doesn't happen quickly or accidentally. Usually it is a process of many decisions to disobey God over a period of time, until a person's faith is finally cooked, much like the proverbial frog in a slowly heated pot of water.

Our Heavenly Father is incredibly patient and loving with His wayward children, but in the end, we still have the freedom to choose to follow Him, or not to follow Him.

Sadly, over time, enough choices to disobey God can harden our heart and leave us distanced and cold toward Him, hardly able to hear His loving voice of conviction. We become very vulnerable to a foolish decision to turn and walk away from Him. If we do this, we are abandoning the eternal security and salvation and blessings that God promises to those who follow Him.

If this message seems odd in your hearing and difficult to believe in light of what you've always thought, I can empathize. It struck me surprising as well, however, there are pages and pages of Scripture that make the subject clear. I encourage you to read some of them in Appendix C.

Here is just one more example of the many Scriptures showing that as believers, we have a *secure position* in Christ as long as we follow Him, however, *that secure position can be lost if we choose again to live our own way.* "Therefore, dear friends, since you have been forewarned, be on your guard so that you may not be carried away by the error of the lawless and *fall from your secure position*" (2Pet 3:17, NIV, emphasis mine).

If you have been walking in sin but you still sense God's conviction to repent, I implore you, please repent now while you can still hear His call! Don't leave your hope based on a false eternal security.

(The subject of endurance and turning from Christ is covered in more detail in the third section of chapter five, and even more eye opening is Appendix C which conveniently provides a large collection of relevant Scripture on the subject.)

Endurance Motivated by Fearful Duty or Passionate Love?

Usually when a beautiful young couple gaze into each other's eyes and vow, "Till death do us part," they do so with thrill and excitement and passionate love, not in *dread* of a long endurance, but in *hope* of one. They look forward to helping each other, romancing each other, caring for each other, blessing each other, forgiving each other with lavish grace, complementing each other, and enjoying each other in intimate and passionate love. As long as this is the tone of their marriage, motivation to endure in marriage will be abundant.

If on the other hand, a couple remains married because they must, or because it is their duty, or because they fear the alternative for their children, or because they are obliged to, then endurance will be possible but much more difficult. When married people have no attraction that draws them close in love, and they are kept together only by the fear of divorce and avoidance of its pain and destruction, every little act of kindness and courtesy becomes a chore of survival and duty. Endurance becomes a painful drudgery, when it could have been an adventure of unending, outrageous love.

Why then, will *you* obey God? Because you have to, in order to avoid His wrath? I have to admit, that's where *I* started. I signed up for fire insurance when I was five. Heaven sounded like a better place than hell, so I chose Christ. But while the fear or respect of God is the beginning of wisdom, it doesn't end there. Salvation is just the beginning!

Becoming a child of God makes you part of the Bride, and this opens the door to a cosmic adventure which involves a marriage to Jesus (Rev 19:6-10)! In other words, the big picture is not 'simply' getting to heaven and then being bored for all eternity...it is about relationship, it is about intimacy, it is about outrageous love, it is about entering into one's destiny, it is about never-ending surprise and joy and discovery. Do you see that this is actually what drives the whole plan? God is not simply looking for servants. He seeks a beautiful and desirable Bride for

His Son.[1] God invites us to come near to Him. If we do, He will come near to us (James 4:8).

And so our repentance and endurance is motivated from *two* directions… we turn FROM, and we turn TO. It is not only about avoiding sin, or avoiding hell, or about hatred of the devil. The other much more powerful side that motivates and propels our endurance, is an attraction to God, a love for Him, an enjoyment of incredible intimacy with Him, a cosmic adventure both now and in Heaven to come!

1.   Reinke, Leslie. Personal email January 13, 2012.

Chapter 10

THE MATHEMATICS OF SALVATION

S ome people like to think mathematically to keep things simple, short and sweet. For them, the salvation equation could be written like this!

The requirements for salvation = (What God did to save us) + (What we must do to be saved)

What God Did to Save Us: He prepared a covering made of His own perfect blood to cover our imperfection so we can become righteous in His sight. This opens up the option of a reconciled relationship with Him as our adopted Father. This required from God: (God's love) + (God's grace) + (God's mercy) + (the shedding of sinless blood which only God's Son, the sinless man Jesus, could do in man's place) + (the resurrection of Jesus) + (God's call to salvation) + (God's forgiveness)

What We Must Do to Be Saved: We must do the will of God the Father who is in heaven
The will of God the Father = (trust His Son Jesus) + (obey His Son Jesus)
= (believe in Jesus) + (repent) + (endure to the end)
To believe in Jesus = (trust Jesus) + (rely upon Jesus) + (adhere to Jesus)
To repent = (change mind) + (change ways) = turning from a life of sin to a life of obedience to God out of love for Him.
Therefore, what we must do to be saved = (trust Jesus) + (rely upon Jesus) + (adhere to Jesus) + (change mind) + (change ways) + (endure to the end)[1]

---

1.   The phrase *adhere to Jesus* is somewhat redundant with the term repent. The terms overlap, where obedience is concerned. Therefore, one could eliminate *adhere to Jesus* from the equation if *repent* is left in, or one could eliminate *repent* if *adhere to Jesus* is retained in the definition of *believe.* I chose to leave both terms in for fullness of meaning.

Chapter 11

THE LORD TEST

This chapter provides the landmark practical application for everything you have read thus far, so let's summarize the book in just three paragraphs before we dive into the practical application. In summary, there are many deceptions in 'Christianity' today which keep people thinking they are saved when they are not. They feel safe, but they are on today's very seductive, very lethal Titanic. They are living in disobedience to the One they call "Lord," foolishly thinking His grace will make up for their lack of repentance. But in reality, the only people who get into heaven are those who *do the will of the Father Who is in heaven.*

What is the Father's will? His will is that I *trust* AND *obey* His Son Jesus. If I don't obey Him by my lifestyle, I'm proving that I don't trust Him, and I'm hell-bound by my own choice. If I want to be saved, I need to obey Jesus and *His* words, and not merely the words of teachers coming in His name who teach their traditions which are often contrary to God's words. Therefore, I must learn God's words through personal study of the Bible and I must choose my spiritual leaders wisely.

It is not my obedience that earns my salvation. Jesus alone earned my salvation. My enduring lifestyle of obedience indicates my faith is in Jesus and my reliance is on what *He* did to save me. If I say I believe in Jesus but I don't obey and follow Him, my faith or belief is at best historical, and at worst, a lie. Either way, it is useless to save me.

What About You?

Have you been unknowingly riding on Today's Titanic? Recently a couple met me after hearing this message and confessed, "We always thought we *were* Christians, but now we know otherwise." They had finally realized the need to obey the one they had been calling Lord!

Have you based your salvation on a faith that *obeys* Jesus, or have you been relying on a false faith that obeys yourself or a religious leader first? Does your belief drive you to search out *God's* words in the Bible to discover *His* will for yourself, or have you been assuming someone else is giving you the true goods? Again, Jesus says, "If the light you think you have is actually darkness, how deep that darkness is!" (Mt 6:23, NLT).

THE LORD TEST –Introduction

Using your imagination, come with me into a virtual reality… Imagine you've died, and you are now in front of Jesus, the Judge of the world. He's the One you've been calling Lord; the One you've prayed to, the One you've believed in, the One you've trusted to save you. Then Jesus looks you in the eye and says with great sadness, "I never knew you; depart from Me, you who act wickedly disregarding My commands" (Mt 7:23).

You're shocked…there must be some mistake! You say, "But Jesus, I trusted in You to save me!"

In utter dismay, you're led down a long dark tunnel toward everlasting doom, your heart racing, and memories of your life flying by. How could this be!? You're stunned. You're horrified! Your heart sinks and sweat beads of terror begin to cover you as the eternal significance of what you've just heard from Jesus sinks in. You begin to examine your life more honestly than ever before…*"Why has this happened? In what ways have I been calling Jesus "Lord" but not obeying Him? How could this rejection and punishment possibly be justified in light of how I've lived my life?"*

This introduces THE LORD TEST. It's a self-examination where you ask those exact questions *now*, so you won't have to ask them *later* when it's too late to change.

The human heart is deceitful. We readily deceive ourselves into thinking we are pretty good. But this is an opportunity to step out of that deception, to examine yourself naked and bare before God, letting Him show you what you really are like. Has He *been* your Lord, or have you only been *calling* Him "Lord"?

"The heart is deceitful above all things, and it is exceedingly perverse and corrupt and severely, mortally sick! Who can know it [perceive, understand, be acquainted with his own heart and mind]?" (Jer 17:9).

Jeremiah exclaims how difficult it is to truthfully know our own heart, due to our deceitfulness. For example, it is so easy to fall into the trap of measuring ourselves according to what is considered normal or acceptable behavior all around us. We can feel especially smug when others don't quite meet the grade we have set for ourselves. That makes us feel even better about ourselves. But now is the time to stop measuring by false standards. Now is the time to measure against *God's* standards. Be brutally honest with yourself. You have nothing to lose, and everything to gain.

> Examine and test and evaluate your own selves to see whether you are holding to your faith and showing the proper fruits of it. Test and prove yourselves [not Christ]. Do you not yourselves realize and know [thoroughly by an ever-increasing experience]

that Jesus Christ is in you--unless you are [counterfeits] disapproved on trial and rejected?

(2Cor 13:5)

I recommend fasting as you talk through THE LORD TEST with God. This exercise will be the hardest for those who have been Christians the longest, but I encourage you to be obedient to the verse just quoted above. You are not exempt from examining yourself. If those whom Jesus sends to hell in Matthew 7 had done this exercise honestly, they could have averted their own destruction. When would you rather ask the hard questions, now or perhaps when it is too late?

For many people, the greatest roadblock to getting saved, is the belief that they already *are* saved. Don't let that be the case for you! Cry out to the Lord in the deepest sincerity, "Jesus Christ of Nazareth, if I don't make changes, am I one of those many who will hear you say, 'I never knew you; depart from Me?' Help me to see truthfully as I examine myself. Help me to see myself in an *accurate* way! Are You really my Lord, or have I just been calling you Lord?"

There are teachers who say we shouldn't question our salvation, but certainly the 'Christians' Jesus sends to hell in Mathew 7 will wish they had questioned and examined theirs! Such advice is contrary to 2Cor 13:5, for how is a person to examine himself to *see if he is in the faith*, if he is not to question his salvation? Is our faith so shaky that it can't even withstand scrutiny?

Such teachers should keep in mind that believing we are saved, isn't what our faith is based on. Our faith is based upon our dependence on what Jesus has done. If that dependence is real, it will be evidenced by our obedience. A person who is convinced he is saved simply because he *believes* he is, will feel shaky about questioning his salvation. This is because he has his faith based on his *hope* rather than on real, honest facts to do with his obeying and trusting Jesus. He is trying to 'hope' his way into heaven. He would be just as well off trying to 'hop' his way into heaven, as trying to 'hope' his way in! We can believe we are saved all we want, but if we aren't saved and we keep believing we are, then all we've done is deceived ourselves.

Believing I'm not sick when I am sick, is to deceive myself and miss out on available help. Believing I have a million dollars in the bank when I don't, is to bring trouble upon myself. Believing I'm saved, when I'm not, is to bring damnation upon myself.

Alternatively, examining myself to see if there is the proper evidence of my being saved, will reveal whether I am or not. The examination doesn't undermine my faith; it only reveals the facts about my condition so I can do something about it if I need to.

As C. H. Spurgeon encouraged, we don't aim to bring doubts and fears through self-examination but rather to drive them away. We don't aim to kill security but rather to kill carnal security. We don't aim to overthrow confidence but rather, fleshly confidence. We don't aim to destroy peace but rather, false peace.[1]

I encourage you to set aside one whole Sunday for THE LORD TEST. Get alone with God, maybe in a hotel or in a secluded park, wherever you would best like to spend time with God with no distractions. Bring your Bible. It's your measuring stick. Pray and fast and ask yourself the questions in THE LORD TEST that follows:

THE LORD TEST
Has Jesus really been my Lord?

(Remember, this evaluation is about the *direction* your life has been headed. It is not about having achieved *perfection*, but about growing in that *direction*. Choose a private place where you can remain undisturbed and undistracted for this special day of fasting, listening, and agreeing with God about all He shows you. All you need is your Bible, this book, a pen with paper, and most importantly, a humble heart. Start by re-reading the preceding introduction to set the stage.)

A Prayer in Deepest Sincerity:

"Jesus Christ of Nazareth, if I don't make changes, am I one of those many people who would hear you say, 'I never knew you; depart from Me, you who act wickedly disregarding My commands'? Help me to see truthfully as I examine myself now. Help me to see myself in an *accurate* way! Help me to understand each Scripture verse below with the understanding you intended. Are You really my Lord, or have I just been calling you "Lord?" In what ways have I been calling You "Lord," but not obeying You?"

Key Points of Examination:

1. Did I take the need for obedience lightly? Did I believe the lie that God is okay with sin since He's gracious and merciful? (Read through Appendix A to determine)

2. Did I work to learn Christ's teachings so I could obey them? (Ps 119:11, 1John 2:3-6)

3. Did I aim to obey His Sermon on the Mount, or was my Christianity patterned more after the status quo? (Mt 5-7)

4. Did I trust my religious leaders without carefully comparing their words to the words of my Heavenly Father? (Deut 4:2, 1Thes 5:20-22, Acts 17:10-11, Ps 119:11)

5. Did I love all believers? Did I hate any? (1John 2:9-11, 1 John 3:10)

6. Did I treasure fellowship with others who love the Lord? (Acts 2:40-47, Heb 10:24-25)

7. Did I hold unforgiveness and resentment toward anyone? (Mt 6:14-15)

8. Did something or someone own me and drive me more than Jesus did? (1John 2:16)

9. Was my life coming to be characterized more by the fruit of the Spirit or by the sinful nature? (Gal 5:16-26)

10. Was there a lack of evidence of the Holy Spirit in my life? If so, did I explain this away even though He was supposed to be evident enough to be a witness confirming my salvation? (2Cor 1:22, 2Tim 3:5, 1Cor 4:20, 1Jn 4:13, Acts 1:8, Acts 5:32)

11. Was my life gaining victory over sin or did I excuse the lack of victory over sin and a backslidden state as normal? (1John 5:2-5)

12. Was I living as any of those listed in 1 Cor 6:9-10 who will not inherit the kingdom of God?

13. Did I live at peace with unconfessed sin? (Is 59:1-2, Eph 4:26-27, Heb 4:16, 1John 1:5-10)

14. Was my hope of salvation based on anything other than my repentance (evidenced by obedience) and faith in Jesus' saving work? (Consider the list of common deceptions in chapter five of this book)

15. Did I give myself more liberty to sin, because of the false security offered by the teaching that guaranteed I couldn't lose my salvation? (Read through Appendix C)

16. Did my heart break over my sin? Did I mourn about the sin in my life and in the world—hating it like God does, or did I laugh at it, live with it, and entertain myself with it? (Mt 5:3-4, Eph 5:11-12)

17. Was I growing to be others-centered and generous, or was I self-centered, spending my time, my talent, and my money on ease and self-gratification? (Mt 25:31-46)

18. Was I growing to have a heart for the lost around me like my Lord does? Was I active in the great commission He gave me? (Mt 28:19-20)

19. Was my life characterized by the description of love in 1Cor13:4-7?

20. Did I love the Lord my God with all my heart, soul, strength and mind? (1Jn 5:3, Lk 10:27)

21. Did I live with the realization of how far I fell short of God's standard and how desperately I needed His grace and mercy? (Mt 5:3)

22. Did I become more like Jesus since calling Him "Lord"? (1Jn 2:6)

THE LORD TEST is over. Has Jesus been Your Lord or do you need to make a significant turn and truly repent? If He *has* been your Lord, what course corrections are needed?

Perhaps God has been opening your eyes to see some things that are making sense like never before! As you welcome God to change your thinking so it lines up with His, the truth will set you free! Now is the time to repent of any wrong thinking and all the sin it has permitted (1John 1:5-10). Now is the time to set a new course, just as a pilot gladly does when he is given updated navigation information!

> God opposes the proud but favors the humble. So humble yourselves before God. Resist the devil, and he will flee from you. Come close to God, and God will come close to you. Wash your hands, you sinners; purify your hearts, for your loyalty is divided between God and the world. Let there be tears for what you have done. Let there be sorrow and deep grief. Let there be sadness instead of laughter, and gloom instead of joy. Humble yourselves before the Lord, and he will lift you up in honor.
>
> (James 4:6-8, NLT)

---

1. Spurgeon, Charles Haddon. "Self Delusion." Need a New Start. 26 Feb 2011. YouTube. 1 Nov 2011. <http://www.youtube.com/watch?v=l0Zj9U0KLCs>

Chapter 12

FOUR SPRINGBOARDS

As you set out to do the will of the Father Who is in heaven—to live a life of obedience and faith in His son Jesus Christ, your most important resource is God's Word the Bible. It's God's instruction manual for life and His love letter to you. And thankfully, His Holy Spirit is your best teacher and your powerful enabler! But where do you start? Here are four springboards to help you get started:

The Sermon on the Mount

Jesus preached a very special sermon up on a mountainside that sums up His teachings and the core teachings of the Bible in an amazing way. It's a great place to start, and you'll find it in Matthew chapters 5-7. It's packed with life-giving insight, and it ends with the warning that we've been looking at—the warning to those calling Him "Lord," who don't obey His words.

The Gospel of Matthew

The Gospel of Matthew tells the story of Jesus' life on earth, and it reveals Him as King of the Kingdom of Heaven! This book is rich with both His teachings and His examples on how to live.

Bible 101

Bible 101 is a free online video course offering a fantastic overview of the Bible starting in Genesis. It brings all the bits and pieces of a person's Bible knowledge together in one easy to see picture! This award-winning course sets you up to feed yourself from the Word with confidence like never before! It is available online at www.GoodSeed.com and on DVD by the title, *The Stranger On the Road to Emmaus*. (See other great resources in Appendix D)

Is Your Parachute On?

As we set out to trust and obey our Lord Jesus, it's very helpful to have a summary understanding of His core message called the "Gospel," together with some background information from the Bible. "Is Your Parachute On?" is exactly that; It is a logical Gospel presentation packed full of key Bible truths. It is a wonderful springboard *into* God's Word because each truth is conveniently followed by its location in the Bible! It is best to get the electronic copy of this so each passage is just a click away! It will be available at www.TodaysTitanic.com. The same resource follows here in printed form:

IS YOUR PARACHUTE ON?

The Bad News First[1]

Statistics show that 10 out of 10 people die. (Now that you're over that shocking news, let's move on.)

After you die, you will be judged by God, (Heb 9:27, 1Pet 4:5, Heb 4:13, Rom 14:11-12) and His judgment is so complete, that He will judge every word, (Mt 12:36-37, Prov 16:2) every thought, and every action of your entire life. (Jer 17:10, 1 Cor 4:5)

> Have you ever lied? (Ex 20:16)
>
> Ever stolen something? (Ex 20:15)
>
> Ever looked at someone lustfully? God calls that adultery. (Ex 20:14, Mt 5:28)
>
> Ever hated someone? God calls that murder. (Ex 20:13, 1Jn 3:15)
>
> Ever used God's name wrongly? (Ex 20:7)
>
> Ever loved something or someone more than God? (1Jn 5:21)
>
> And have you ever not done the things that you should do? (James 4:17)

If you have sinned just once, you have broken God's law, (Rom 3:20, 23, James 2:10) and if you die in your sins, God will be forced to find you guilty, because He is a good and fair judge. (Rom 6:23, Jn 8:24)

Just like a good judge on earth sentences those he finds guilty, (Jer 11:20, 1 Thes 1:5-7) God is also a good judge and must punish sinners and sentence them to prison. (Mt 22:13-14)

—the difference is, this prison is a death sentence forever in a lake of fire called hell. (2 Thes 1:8-9, Rev 20:15)

God often warns of His eternal wrath for those who choose to live in sin. (Mk 9:43-48, Rev 21:8)

The Good News

The good news is, God loves you and He doesn't want anyone to perish in hell. (Jn 3:16, 2Pet 3:9)

Hell was actually prepared for the devil and his demons. (Mt 25:41)

God desires a restored loving relationship with you. (Rom 5:8-11, Rev 19:7-8, Col 1:20-22)

If you choose to turn from your sin and live God's way, (Luke 13:3, Mt 7:21, Acts 17:30, Rev 22:14, Titus 3:5)

He allows your guilt and death sentence to be paid by a substitute! This substitute is God's own Son Jesus Christ, who came to earth in the form of a man. (Rom 5:8-11, Jn 1:14, Jn 3:16, Eph 2:8-9)

He never sinned, yet he sacrificed His life and blood by dying on the cross, (1Jn 3:5, Mt 27:26-65)

in order to save you from having to pay the death penalty yourself. (Rom 4:25, Jn 3:16)

If you turn from your sin to follow God, trusting in the sacrifice of His Son Jesus to save you, then Jesus, whom God raised from the dead, pays the death sentence that you are due to pay yourself for all eternity in hell. (Acts 20:21, Mark 16:16, 1Jn 2:3,4, 1 Cor 15:3-8)

You wouldn't jump out of an airplane without a parachute! Don't plunge into eternity without Jesus as your Savior.

Now is the time to put on your parachute. You are not guaranteed another minute of life! (2 Cor 6:2)

God hasn't given us five or ten different parachutes to choose from. He's given us only one...His Son Jesus Christ. In order to trick us, the devil produces many other ways that seem right called religions, (Jn 8:42-47) religions of wrong gods, (Eph 2:8-10, Gal 3:1-14) religions of works, (Prov 14:12) other ways that seem right

But God says of His Son Jesus Christ, there is no other name given to men by which you may be saved. (Acts 4:12, Jn 14:6)

To avoid eternal punishment with the devil in hell, and to begin a beautiful relationship with God who made you and loves you:

1. Turn from your sinful ways and live God's way. Follow his Son. In joyful repentance, you get to drop your old empty ways for a new life of intimacy with your Creator! (Lk 13:3, Jn 6:29, Jn 6:47, Lk 10:27, Jn 14:23, Rom 8:13-17, 1 Cor 13)

2. Learn what God expects by reading the Bible and listening to His Spirit. (2 Tim 3:16, Lk 6:46-49, Mt 7:21, Ps 119:11, 1Jn 2:3-4)

3. Find other people you can walk with who love Jesus and who actually obey His teachings. (Heb 10:24-25)

4. Be baptized in Jesus' name. (Acts 2:38, Mark 16:16)

5. Share the 'bad news' and the 'good news' with others! (Mt 28:19-20)

---

1. This presentation inspired by: Comfort, Ray. "Hell's Best Kept Secret." Sermon. 2006. livingwaters.com. 13 April 2010.

Two Unusual Invitations

In many books, the appendix is an add-on, but in this book, the first three appendices are actually the foundation of the book. They contain the very words of God that the book results from. For this reason, I specially invite you to read the appendices of this book. They are the words of God that surprised me and gave my theology a much needed shaking.

This book has been published through the generous gifts of people who want the message of Christ to be clearly and accurately proclaimed around the world in an uncompromised way. If that describes you, please enable it's further publication in other languages and in other media forms. Your gifts can be processed by contacting us at: info@todaystitanic.com

Appendix A

SCRIPTURE THAT REVEALS THE CRUCIAL ROLE OF OBEDIENCE FOR SALVATION, AND THE DAMNING CONSEQUENCES OF SIN—EVEN IN THE LIFE OF A 'CHRISTIAN'

Today, many people who call Jesus their Lord live in sin but feel assured Jesus will forgive them when it's all said and done. They are convinced they are saved and that God won't punish them for their sin because Jesus paid it all. They often think things like, "I'm a Christian, so Jesus has already forgiven me for all my sins, past, present and future!" They don't realize the crucial role that obedience has in *obtaining* and *retaining* such a salvation. Some even dismiss talk of repentance and obedience as if it were *legalism* or *salvation by works*, but nothing could be further from the truth.

The following passages of Scripture contrast sharply with the idea that Christians can live a lifestyle of sin and hope to be saved. They remind us that there is a very important "if...then" aspect to the salvation equation.

Note: Scripture is listed in the order found in the Bible.

If we obey, God preserves us.	And the Lord commanded us to observe all these statutes, to fear the Lord our God, for our good always, that He might preserve us alive, as *it is* this day. Deut 6:24 NKJV
God's favor and blessings result from obedience while curses result from disobedience—a general principle throughout Scripture. (See also Mt 25:41)	**1** "If you indeed obey the Lord your God and are careful to observe all his commandments I am giving you today, the Lord your God will elevate you above all the nations of the earth. **5** "But if you ignore the Lord your God and are not careful to keep all his commandments and statutes I am giving you today, then all these curses will come upon you in full force: Deut 28:1,5 NET
Death is the result of sin. In this case, death was almost immediate.	Nevertheless, because by this deed you have utterly scorned the Lord and given great occasion to the enemies of the Lord to blaspheme, the child that is born to you shall surely die. 2Sam 12:14
Obedience results in blessing. Disobedience results in the blessing being revoked.	**4** Now if you walk before Me as your father David walked, in integrity of heart and in uprightness, to do according to all that I have commanded you, *and* if you keep My statutes and My judgments, **5** then I will establish the throne of your kingdom over Israel forever, as I promised David your father, saying, 'You shall not fail to have a man on the throne of Israel.' **6** *But* if you or your sons at all turn from following Me, and do not keep My commandments *and* My statutes which I have set before you, but go and serve other gods and worship them, **7** then I will cut off Israel from the land which I have given them; and this house which I have consecrated for My name I will cast out of My sight. Israel will be a proverb and a byword among all peoples. 1 Kings 9:4-7 NKJV
Continuous obedience is the condition for many of God's blessings.	I will establish his kingdom forever if he loyally and continuously obeys My commandments and My ordinances, as he does today. 1 Chronicles 28:7

Repentance resulting in obedience is always the condition for forgiveness of sin.	If My people, who are called by My name, shall humble themselves, pray, seek, crave, and require of necessity My face and turn from their wicked ways, then will I hear from heaven, forgive their sin, and heal their land. 2Chr 7:14
Forsake God and eventually He will forsake you.	Then the Spirit of God came upon Zechariah son of Jehoiada the priest, who stood over the people, and he said to them, Thus says God: Why do you transgress the commandments of the Lord so that you cannot prosper? Because you have forsaken the Lord, He also has forsaken you. 2Chr 24:20
Repentance is where revival begins.	And the Israelites separated themselves from all foreigners and stood and confessed their sins and the iniquities of their fathers. Neh 9:2
Christians are not exempt.	Boasters can have no standing in Your sight; You abhor all evildoers. Ps 5:5
David is concerned about being cast from God's presence due to his sin.	Cast me not away from Your presence and take not Your Holy Spirit from me. Ps 51:11
Sin hinders our prayers. (See also James 5:16b-17 & 1Pet 3:12 & Is 59:1-2)	If I regard iniquity in my heart, the Lord will not hear me; Psalm 66:18
God's mercy and loving-kindness is reserved for those who worshipfully fear and obey Him.	17But the mercy and loving-kindness of the Lord are from everlasting to everlasting upon those who reverently and worshipfully fear Him, and His righteousness is to children's children—18To such as keep His covenant [hearing, receiving, loving, and obeying it] and to those who [earnestly] remember His commandments to do them [imprinting them on their hearts]. Ps 103:17-18
God has a special love for those who love Him.	I love those who love me, and those who seek me early and diligently shall find me. Prov 8:17

We reap what we sow.	The backslider in heart [from God and from fearing God] shall be filled with [the fruit of] his own ways, and a good man shall be satisfied with [the fruit of] his ways [with the holy thoughts and actions which his heart prompts and in which he delights]. Prov 14:14
The religious practices of those living in sin are exceedingly offensive to God.	The sacrifice of the wicked is an abomination, hateful and exceedingly offensive to the Lord, but the prayer of the upright is His delight! Prov 15:8
Some people think they are clean while in God's eyes they are filthy.	There is a class of people who are pure in their own eyes, and yet are not washed from their own filth. Prov 30:12
God is just and gives to each according to his deeds.	I the Lord search the mind, I try the heart, even to give to every man according to his ways, according to the fruit of his doings. Jer 17:10
Turn. Turn. Turn and live! Or continue in sin and die.	Say to them, As I live, says the Lord God, I have no pleasure in the death of the wicked, but rather that the wicked turn from his way and live. Turn back, turn back from your evil ways, for why will you die, O house of Israel? Ezek 33:11
Obedience is key in our relationship with God.	My God will cast them away because they did not listen to and obey Him, and they shall be wanderers and fugitives among the nations. Hosea 9:17
Acting as if God is fine with people living in sin, and saying that He delights in them while they do so, is tiresome to the Lord. (Such perverted grace is popular today.)	You have wearied the Lord with your words. Yet you say, In what way have we wearied Him? [You do it when by your actions] you say, Everyone who does evil is good in the sight of the Lord and He delights in them. Or [by asking], Where is the God of justice? Mal 2:17

If my life doesn't prove my change of heart, then I'm like these people whom John called vipers! The final end of such people is fire.	7 But when he saw many Pharisees and Sadducees coming to his baptism, he said to them, "You offspring of vipers! Who warned you to flee from the coming wrath? 8 Therefore produce fruit that proves your repentance, 9 and don't think you can say to yourselves, 'We have Abraham as our father.' For I tell you that God can raise up children for Abraham from these stones! 10 Even now the ax is laid at the root of the trees, and every tree that does not produce good fruit will be cut down and thrown into the fire. Mt 3:7-10 NET
Jesus clarifies that our salvation hinges on a certain level of *our* righteousness, a level of obedience greater than the Pharisees and scribes. (Our righteousness doesn't *earn* our salvation, but it is evidence of the faith that *engages Christ's* righteousness on our behalf. In a similar way, we use a *little power* to move a gearshift in order to *engage* the *great power* of an engine to move our car, though it is not our power that moves the car.) (See also James 2:24)	For I tell you, unless your righteousness (your uprightness and your right standing with God) is more than that of the scribes and Pharisees, you will never enter the kingdom of heaven. Mt 5:20

Profession of faith in Jesus as Lord, without *obedience* to Him as Lord, leads to a horrific surprise at the end of life and great destruction.	21Not everyone who says to Me, Lord, Lord, will enter the kingdom of heaven, but he who does the will of My Father Who is in heaven. 22Many will say to Me on that day, Lord, Lord, have we not prophesied in Your name and driven out demons in Your name and done many mighty works in Your name? 23And then I will say to them openly (publicly), I never knew you; depart from Me, you who act wickedly [disregarding My commands]. 24So everyone who hears these words of Mine and acts upon them [obeying them] will be like a sensible (prudent, practical, wise) man who built his house upon the rock. 25And the rain fell and the floods came and the winds blew and beat against that house; yet it did not fall, because it had been founded on the rock. 26And everyone who hears these words of Mine and does not do them will be like a stupid (foolish) man who built his house upon the sand. 27And the rain fell and the floods came and the winds blew and beat against that house, and it fell--and great and complete was the fall of it. Mt 7:21-27
Endurance is required to secure salvation. No one can rest assured on a one-time salvation event if he is not persevering.	And you will be hated by all for My name's sake, but he who perseveres and endures to the end will be saved [from spiritual disease and death in the world to come]. Mt 10:22

Our actions count more than our words. True belief in Jesus is visible in our actions. True belief in Jesus adheres to and obeys Him.	28 "What do you think? A man had two sons. He went to the first and said, 'Son, go and work in the vineyard today.' 29 The boy answered, 'I will not.' But later he had a change of heart and went. 30 The father went to the other son and said the same thing. This boy answered, 'I will, sir,' but did not go. 31 Which of the two did his father's will?" They said, "The first." Jesus said to them, "I tell you the truth, tax collectors and prostitutes will go ahead of you into the kingdom of God! 32 For John came to you in the way of righteousness, and you did not believe him. But the tax collectors and prostitutes did believe. Although you saw this, you did not later change your minds and believe him. Mt 21:28-32 NET
Endurance is required to secure salvation. No one can rest assured on a one-time salvation event if he is not persevering.	11 Then many false prophets will rise up and deceive many. 12 And because lawlessness will abound, the love of many will grow cold. 13 But he who endures to the end shall be saved. Mt 24:11-13 NKJV
Pretenders wind up in hell.	And will punish him [cut him up by scourging] and put him with the pretenders (hypocrites); there will be weeping and grinding of teeth. Mt 24:51
The ultimate curse of disobedience is eternal fire.	41 "Then he will say to those on his left, 'Depart from me, you accursed, into the eternal fire that has been prepared for the devil and his angels! 42 For I was hungry and you gave me nothing to eat, I was thirsty and you gave me nothing to drink. Mt 25:41-42 NET
The accurate Gospel demands *faith* AND *conduct* changing repentance.	And saying, The [appointed period of] time is fulfilled (completed), and the kingdom of God is at hand; repent (have a change of mind which issues in regret for past sins and in change of conduct for the better) and believe (trust in, rely on, and adhere to) the good news (the Gospel). Mark 1:15

*Repentance involves not only a change of *mind* but also a change of *way*.	So they went out and preached that men should repent [that they should change their minds for the better and heartily amend their ways, with abhorrence of their past sins]. Mark 6:12
The Father expects us to obey His Son.	And a cloud threw a shadow upon them, and a voice came out of the cloud, saying, This is My Son, the [most dearworthy] Beloved One. Be constantly listening to and obeying Him! Mark 9:7
Saving belief includes adherence to Jesus and His message, without which comes condemnation.	He who believes [who adheres to and trusts in and relies on the Gospel and Him Whom it sets forth] and is baptized will be saved [from the penalty of eternal death]; but he who does not believe [who does not adhere to and trust in and rely on the Gospel and Him Whom it sets forth] will be condemned. Mark 16:16
Calling Jesus "Lord" without obeying Him as Lord has disastrous consequences.	**46** "Why do you call me 'Lord, Lord,' and don't do what I tell you?**47** "Everyone who comes to me and listens to my words and puts them into practice – I will show you what he is like: **48** He is like a man building a house, who dug down deep, and laid the foundation on bedrock. When a flood came, the river burst against that house but could not shake it, because it had been well built. **49** But the person who hears and does not put my words into practice is like a man who built a house on the ground without a foundation. When the river burst against that house, it collapsed immediately, and was utterly destroyed!" Luke 6:46-49 NET
Every true Christian is on a path that conforms to Christ's example.	And He said to all, If any person wills to come after Me, let him deny himself [disown himself, forget, lose sight of himself and his own interests, refuse and give up himself] and take up his cross daily and follow Me [cleave steadfastly to Me, conform wholly to My example in living and, if need be, in dying also]. Luke 9:23

Loving God is the way to the Kingdom of God. Loving God requires obeying Him. Therefore, we must obey God if we hope to enter the Kingdom of heaven. (See also John 14:23)	**27**And he replied, You must love the Lord your God with all your heart and with all your soul and with all your strength and with all your mind; and your neighbor as yourself. **28**And Jesus said to him, You have answered correctly; do this, and you will live [enjoy active, blessed, endless life in the kingdom of God]. Luke 10:27-28
Jesus can't make it any clearer. Repent (change your *mind* and *ways*) or perish.	I tell you, No; but unless you repent (change your mind for the better and heartily amend your ways, with abhorrence of your past sins), you will all likewise perish and be lost eternally. Luke 13:3
Faith and obedience isn't an easy thing. It takes effort. Many fail who try.	Strive to enter by the narrow door [force yourselves through it], for many, I tell you, will try to enter and will not be able. Luke 13:24
Repentance is the condition that must be met for forgiveness of sins.	**46**And said to them, Thus it is written that the Christ (the Messiah) should suffer and on the third day rise from (among) the dead, **47**And that repentance [with a view to and as the condition of] forgiveness of sins should be preached in His name to all nations, beginning from Jerusalem. Luke 24:46-47
Belief that saves, means trusting Him, clinging to Him, and relying on Him.	For God so greatly loved and dearly prized the world that He [even] gave up His only begotten (unique) Son, so that whoever believes in (trusts in, clings to, relies on) Him shall not perish (come to destruction, be lost) but have eternal (everlasting) life. John 3:16
Believe (trust and obey) to be saved. The opposite of believing is disobeying, which results in death.	And he who believes in (has faith in, clings to, relies on) the Son has (now possesses) eternal life. But whoever disobeys (is unbelieving toward, refuses to trust in, disregards, is not subject to) the Son will never see (experience) life, but [instead] the wrath of God abides on him. [God's displeasure remains on him; His indignation hangs over him continually.] John 3:36

Stop sinning (repent and obey) or something worse may happen to you. (Something far worse, forever)	Afterward, when Jesus found him in the temple, He said to him, See, you are well! Stop sinning or something worse may happen to you. John 5:14
Belief that saves, is belief that clings to and relies on Jesus, not belief that disregards His commandments and stays distant.	I assure you, most solemnly I tell you, the person whose ears are open to My words [who listens to My message] and believes and trusts in and clings to and relies on Him Who sent Me has (possesses now) eternal life. And he does not come into judgment [does not incur sentence of judgment, will not come under condemnation], but he has already passed over out of death into life. John 5:24
Belief that saves, adheres to Jesus.	I assure you, most solemnly I tell you, he who believes in Me [who adheres to, trusts in, relies on, and has faith in Me] has (now possesses) eternal life. John 6:47
A mere historical belief in Jesus doesn't cut it. Jesus' brothers had that much...they had no doubt of His existence, but they are called unbelievers.	For [even] His brothers did not believe in or adhere to or trust in or rely on Him either. John 7:5
Death results if you do not adhere to, trust in, and rely on Jesus.	That is why I told you that you will die in (under the curse of) your sins; for if you do not believe that I am He [Whom I claim to be--if you do not adhere to, trust in, and rely on Me], you will die in your sins. John 8:24
True disciples hold fast to His teaching.	So Jesus said to those Jews who had believed in Him, If you abide in My word [hold fast to My teachings and live in accordance with them], you are truly My disciples. John 8:31

Believing means adhering to and trusting and relying on Him... not just relying on Him for salvation.	DO NOT let your hearts be troubled (distressed, agitated). You believe in and adhere to and trust in and rely on God; believe in and adhere to and trust in and rely also on Me. John 14:1
Real love for Jesus involves obeying Him. (See also Luke 10:27-28)	Jesus answered, If a person [really] loves Me, he will keep My word [obey My teaching]; and My Father will love him, and We will come to him and make Our home (abode, special dwelling place) with him. John 14:23
Dwelling in Jesus demands obeying Him and enduring. If we keep His commandments we stay on in His love. If we don't, our end is separation from Him and fire.	4Dwell in Me, and I will dwell in you. [Live in Me, and I will live in you.] Just as no branch can bear fruit of itself without abiding in (being vitally united to) the vine, neither can you bear fruit unless you abide in Me. 5I am the Vine; you are the branches. Whoever lives in Me and I in him bears much (abundant) fruit. However, apart from Me [cut off from vital union with Me] you can do nothing. 6If a person does not dwell in Me, he is thrown out like a [broken-off] branch, and withers; such branches are gathered up and thrown into the fire, and they are burned. 10If you keep My commandments [if you continue to obey My instructions], you will abide in My love and live on in it, just as I have obeyed My Father's commandments and live on in His love. John 15:4-6, 10
Repenting includes a revolutionary life change to align with God's will. It's required for forgiveness of sins.	And Peter answered them, Repent (change your views and purpose to accept the will of God in your inner selves instead of rejecting it) and be baptized, every one of you, in the name of Jesus Christ for the forgiveness of and release from your sins; and you shall receive the gift of the Holy Spirit. Acts 2:38
A change of mind and purpose in agreement with God is the basic requirement for forgiveness of sin.	So repent (change your mind and purpose); turn around and return [to God], that your sins may be erased (blotted out, wiped clean), that times of refreshing (of recovering from the effects of heat, of reviving with fresh air) may come from the presence of the Lord; Acts 3:19

Sin leads to death even in the New Testament church. In this case, lying to God brought death to both husband and wife immediately.	10Immediately she fell down at his feet and breathed her last. When the young men came in they found her dead, and they carried her out and buried her beside her husband. 11And great fear came upon the whole church and upon all who heard of these things. Acts 5:10-11
Saving belief involves being devoted to Jesus and all He stands for.	More and more there were being added to the Lord those who believed [those who acknowledged Jesus as their Savior and devoted themselves to Him joined and gathered with them], crowds both of men and of women, Acts 5:14
Repentance is a must. It includes such a hearty turning that we abhor our past sins.	Such [former] ages of ignorance God, it is true, ignored and allowed to pass unnoticed; but now He charges all people everywhere to repent (to change their minds for the better and heartily to amend their ways, with abhorrence of their past sins), Acts 17:30
Repentance AND *faith* in Jesus was Paul's main message. Not just one or the other.	But constantly and earnestly I bore testimony both to Jews and Greeks, urging them to turn in repentance [that is due] to God and to have faith in our Lord Jesus Christ [that is due Him]. Acts 20:21
The gospel Paul preached required repentance in an ongoing sense.	But made known openly first of all to those at Damascus, then at Jerusalem and throughout the whole land of Judea, and also among the Gentiles, that they should repent and turn to God, and do works and live lives consistent with and worthy of their repentance. Acts 26:20
Those who call Jesus their Lord are not exempt from this truth.	7 To those who by persistence in doing good seek glory, honor and immortality, he will give eternal life. 8 But for those who are self-seeking and who reject the truth and follow evil, there will be wrath and anger. Rom 2:7-8NIV
Those who obey God's Law are the ones considered righteous by God.	13For it is not merely hearing the Law [read] that makes one righteous before God, but it is the doers of the Law who will be held guiltless and acquitted and justified. Rom 2:13

Obedience doesn't *earn* us a right standing with God, but it *leads us to* a right standing with God. We get this right standing as a free gift through faith in Jesus Christ's perfect blood, shed for us. The wages of sin is STILL death. This is what unrepentant people earn whether or not they call themselves *Christians*. The free gift of God is not for the unrepentant, but for those who have become obedient "servants of righteousness" conforming to God's will.	15 What then? Shall we sin because we are not under law but under grace? Absolutely not! 16 Do you not know that if you present yourselves as obedient slaves, you are slaves of the one you obey, either of sin resulting in death, or obedience resulting in righteousness? 17 But thanks be to God that though you were slaves to sin, you obeyed from the heart that pattern of teaching you were entrusted to, 18 and having been freed from sin, you became enslaved to righteousness. 19 (I am speaking in human terms because of the weakness of your flesh.) For just as you once presented your members as slaves to impurity and lawlessness leading to more lawlessness, so now present your members as slaves to righteousness leading to sanctification. 20 For when you were slaves of sin, you were free with regard to righteousness. 21 So what benefit did you then reap from those things that you are now ashamed of? For the end of those things is death. 22 But now, freed from sin and enslaved to God, you have your benefit leading to sanctification, and the end is eternal life. 23 For the payoff of sin is death, but the gift of God is eternal life in Christ Jesus our Lord. Rom 6:15-23 NET
Living in sin results in death. Living in obedience results in life forever as children of God.	13 (for if you live according to the flesh, you will die), but if by the Spirit you put to death the deeds of the body you will live. 14 For all who are led by the Spirit of God are the sons of God. 15 For you did not receive the spirit of slavery leading again to fear, but you received the Spirit of adoption, by whom we cry, "Abba, Father." 16 The Spirit himself bears witness to our spirit that we are God's children. 17 And if children, then heirs (namely, heirs of God and also fellow heirs with Christ) – if indeed we suffer with him so we may also be glorified with him. Rom 8:13-17 NET

(Today we hear a lot about God's gracious kindness and less about His severity, but both are equally real.) His grace and kindness is for those who *continue* and *abide* in it. This endurance is a choice, just like initial repentance is a choice. Being cut off is the alternative to enduring.	Then note and appreciate the gracious kindness and the severity of God: severity toward those who have fallen, but God's gracious kindness to you-- provided you continue in His grace and abide in His kindness; otherwise you too will be cut off (pruned away). Rom 11:22
Greed and other common sins are considered so serious that we are to disassociate with such unrepentant persons who behave these ways yet bear the name *Christian*.	But now I write to you not to associate with anyone who bears the name of [Christian] brother if he is known to be guilty of immorality or greed, or is an idolater [whose soul is devoted to any object that usurps the place of God], or is a person with a foul tongue [railing, abusing, reviling, slandering], or is a drunkard or a swindler or a robber. [No] you must not so much as eat with such a person. 1Cor 5:11
Unrighteous "Christians" don't make it. Don't be deceived by those who say they do.	Do you not know that the unrighteous and the wrongdoers will not inherit or have any share in the kingdom of God? Do not be deceived (misled): neither the impure and immoral, nor idolaters, nor adulterers, nor those who participate in homosexuality, 1Cor 6:9
Keeping this temporary religious law counts for nothing, but keeping God's eternal commandments is what counts.	For circumcision is nothing and counts for nothing, neither does uncircumcision, but [what counts is] keeping the commandments of God. 1Cor 7:19

Even Paul realizes he could walk away from salvation and be rejected if he didn't choose to persevere.	But [like a boxer] I buffet my body [handle it roughly, discipline it by hardships] and subdue it, for fear that after proclaiming to others the Gospel and things pertaining to it, I myself should become unfit [not stand the test, be unapproved and rejected as a counterfeit]. 1Cor 9:27
The death that disobedient Israel earned in the wilderness, serves to warn us against disobedience today. If we choose disobedience, we can expect the same result they got—death. Sin is still just as venomous and serious to God on this side of the cross as it was on the other side of the cross. (See also Heb 4:11 & Jude 1:4-5)	**5** But God was not pleased with most of them, for they were cut down in the wilderness. **6** These things happened as examples for us, so that we will not crave evil things as they did. **7** So do not be idolaters, as some of them were. As it is written, *"The people sat down to eat and drink and rose up to play."* **8** And let us not be immoral, as some of them were, and twenty-three thousand died in a single day. **9** And let us not put Christ to the test, as some of them did, and were destroyed by snakes. **10** And do not complain, as some of them did, and were killed by the destroying angel. **11** These things happened to them as examples and were written for our instruction, on whom the ends of the ages have come. **12** So let the one who thinks he is standing be careful that he does not fall. 1Cor 10:5-12 NET
Endurance is required to secure salvation. No one can rest assured on a one-time salvation event if he is not persevering.	**1** Now, brothers and sisters, I want to remind you of the gospel I preached to you, which you received and on which you have taken your stand. **2** By this gospel you are saved, if you hold firmly to the word I preached to you. Otherwise, you have believed in vain.1Cor 15:1-2 NIV
Christians are not exempt from this warning.	**19** The acts of the flesh are obvious: sexual immorality, impurity and debauchery; **20** idolatry and witchcraft; hatred, discord, jealousy, fits of rage, selfish ambition, dissensions, factions **21** and envy; drunkenness, orgies, and the like. I warn you, as I did before, that those who live like this will not inherit the kingdom of God. Gal 5:19-21 NIV

God won't be mocked by those hoping to fool Him with mere professions of faith.	Do not be deceived and deluded and misled; God will not allow Himself to be sneered at (scorned, disdained, or mocked by mere pretensions or professions, or by His precepts being set aside.) [He inevitably deludes himself who attempts to delude God.] For whatever a man sows, that and that only is what he will reap. Galatians 6:7
The unrepentant have no inheritance in the kingdom of heaven. No inheritance in the kingdom of God due to greed, impure thoughts, etc.	3But immorality (sexual vice) and all impurity [of lustful, rich, wasteful living] or greediness must not even be named among you, as is fitting and proper among saints (God's consecrated people). 4Let there be no filthiness (obscenity, indecency) nor foolish and sinful (silly and corrupt) talk, nor coarse jesting, which are not fitting or becoming; but instead voice your thankfulness [to God]. 5For be sure of this: that no person practicing sexual vice or impurity in thought or in life, or one who is covetous [who has lustful desire for the property of others and is greedy for gain]--for he [in effect] is an idolater--has any inheritance in the kingdom of Christ and of God. 6Let no one delude and deceive you with empty excuses and groundless arguments [for these sins], for through these things the wrath of God comes upon the sons of rebellion and disobedience. Eph 5:3-6
Suffering and punishment of everlasting ruin goes to those who refuse to obey the Gospel of Christ.	8To deal out retribution (chastisement and vengeance) upon those who do not know or perceive or become acquainted with God, and [upon those] who ignore and refuse to obey the Gospel of our Lord Jesus Christ. 9Such people will pay the penalty and suffer the punishment of everlasting ruin (destruction and perdition) and eternal exclusion and banishment from the presence of the Lord and from the glory of His power, 2Thes 1:6-9
Disassociate from unrepentant people in the church. (See also 1Cor 5:11)	But if anyone [in the church] refuses to obey what we say in this letter, take note of that person and do not associate with him, so that he may be ashamed. 2Thes 3:14

Fleeing from evil is what happens as we repent and run toward God.	But as for you, O man of God, flee from all these things; aim at and pursue righteousness (right standing with God and true goodness), godliness (which is the loving fear of God and being Christlike), faith, love, steadfastness (patience), and gentleness of heart. 1Tim 6:11
Genuine faith and false faith are visibly distinguished by conduct. Avoid people of false faith.	For [although] they hold a form of piety (true religion), they deny and reject and are strangers to the power of it [their conduct belies the genuineness of their profession]. Avoid [all] such people [turn away from them]. 2Tim 3:5
God won't be fooled. He knows who are His—those who aim to stand far from sin.	Nevertheless, God's solid foundation stands firm, sealed with this inscription: "The Lord knows those who are his," and, "Everyone who confesses the name of the Lord must turn away from wickedness. 2Tim 2:19NIV
They claim to know God, but by their actions they deny Him. Disobedience is akin to unbelief.	They profess to know God [to recognize, perceive, and be acquainted with Him], but deny and disown and renounce Him by what they do; they are detestable and loathsome, unbelieving and disobedient and disloyal and rebellious, and [they are] unfit and worthless for good work (deed or enterprise) of any kind. Titus 1:16
Endurance is required to secure salvation. No one can rest assured on a one-time salvation event if he is not persevering.	But Christ (the Messiah) was faithful over His [own Father's] house as a Son [and Master of it]. And it is we who are [now members] of this house, if we hold fast and firm to the end our joyful and exultant confidence and sense of triumph in our hope [in Christ]. Heb 3:6
Endurance is required to secure salvation. No one can rest assured on a one-time salvation event if he is not persevering.	For we have become fellows with Christ (the Messiah) and share in all He has for us, if only we hold our first newborn confidence and original assured expectation [in virtue of which we are believers] firm and unshaken to the end. Heb 3:14

Obedience takes diligent effort. It is as crucial today as it was in Moses' day, while disobedience has similar consequences as it did then. (See also 1Cor 10:5-12 & Jude 1:4-5)	Let us therefore be zealous and exert ourselves and strive diligently to enter that rest [of God, to know and experience it for ourselves], that no one may fall or perish by the same kind of unbelief and disobedience [into which those in the wilderness fell]. Heb 4:11
Jesus saves those who give heed and obey Him, not those who don't.	And, [His completed experience] making Him perfectly [equipped], He became the Author and Source of eternal salvation to all those who give heed and obey Him, Heb 5:9
Repentance is the first of the most elementary teachings of Christ.	Therefore let us move beyond the elementary teachings about Christ and be taken forward to maturity, not laying again the foundation of repentance from acts that lead to death, and of faith in God, Heb 6:1 NIV
Without holiness no one will ever see the Lord. Obeying Jesus leads to having His holiness applied to our account.	Strive to live in peace with everybody and pursue that consecration and holiness without which no one will [ever] see the Lord. Heb 12:14
It's dangerously easy to deceive ourselves in order to excuse our disobedience.	But be doers of the Word [obey the message], and not merely listeners to it, betraying yourselves [into deception by reasoning contrary to the Truth]. James 1:22

Faith without actions of obedience is dead and unable to save our souls.

Real faith doesn't exist without real works, because real faith isn't merely something internal. It is something active.

Verse 24—Our justification (being pronounced righteous before God) is dependent on our obedience, in so much as it is our obedience that allows Christ's perfection to be applied to our account. This isn't to say our obedience or good works *earns* our salvation, but that our obedience accompanies any true faith in Jesus. It remains 100% the work of Jesus to cover us in His righteousness as a result of this true active faith. (See also Mt 5:20)

14 What good is it, my brothers and sisters, if someone claims to have faith but has no deeds? Can such faith save them? **15** Suppose a brother or a sister is without clothes and daily food. **16** If one of you says to them, "Go in peace; keep warm and well fed," but does nothing about their physical needs, what good is it? **17** In the same way, faith by itself, if it is not accompanied by action, is dead. **18** But someone will say, "You have faith; I have deeds." Show me your faith without deeds, and I will show you my faith by my deeds. **19** You believe that there is one God. Good! Even the demons believe that—and shudder. **20** You foolish person, do you want evidence that faith without deeds is useless? **21** Was not our father Abraham considered righteous for what he did when he offered his son Isaac on the altar? **22** You see that his faith and his actions were working together, and his faith was made complete by what he did. **23** And the scripture was fulfilled that says, "Abraham believed God, and it was credited to him as righteousness," and he was called God's friend. **24** You see that a person is considered righteous by what they do and not by faith alone. **25** In the same way, was not even Rahab the prostitute considered righteous for what she did when she gave lodging to the spies and sent them off in a different direction? **26** As the body without the spirit is dead, so faith without deeds is dead. James 2:14-26 NIV

God patiently calls us to repentance when we waver.	Come close to God and He will come close to you. [Recognize that you are] sinners, get your soiled hands clean; [realize that you have been disloyal] wavering individuals with divided interests, and purify your hearts [of your spiritual adultery]. James 4:8
The prayers of a *righteous* man have great influence. Not so the prayers of a wicked man. (See also Psalm 66:18 and 1Pet 3:12)	The earnest (heartfelt, continued) prayer of a righteous man makes tremendous power available [dynamic in its working].Elijah was a human being with a nature such as we have [with feelings, affections, and a constitution like ours]; and he prayed earnestly for it not to rain, and no rain fell on the earth for three years and six months. James 5:16b-17
Righteous people are blessed with God's ear and favor, while unrighteous people encounter His opposition. (See also Psalm 66:18 and James 5:16b-17)	For the eyes of the Lord are upon the righteous (those who are upright and in right standing with God), and His ears are attentive to their prayer. But the face of the Lord is against those who practice evil [to oppose them, to frustrate, and defeat them]. 1Pet 3:12
God is extraordinarily patient. He does not desire our punishment, but rather our repentance and eternal life.	The Lord does not delay and is not tardy or slow about what He promises, according to some people's conception of slowness, but He is long-suffering (extraordinarily patient) toward you, not desiring that any should perish, but that all should turn to repentance. 2Pet 3:9

Are you a true Christian? You know you are a Christian if you learn and practice Christ's teachings. If we say we know Him but we don't obey His teachings, we are liars. True Christians ought to conduct themselves as Jesus did.	3And this is how we may discern [daily, by experience] that we are coming to know Him [to perceive, recognize, understand, and become better acquainted with Him]: if we keep (bear in mind, observe, practice) His teachings (precepts, commandments). 4Whoever says, I know Him [I perceive, recognize, understand, and am acquainted with Him] but fails to keep and obey His commandments (teachings) is a liar, and the Truth [of the Gospel] is not in him. 5But he who keeps (treasures) His Word [who bears in mind His precepts, who observes His message in its entirety], truly in him has the love of and for God been perfected (completed, reached maturity). By this we may perceive (know, recognize, and be sure) that we are in Him: 6Whoever says he abides in Him ought [as a personal debt] to walk and conduct himself in the same way in which He walked and conducted Himself. 1Jn 2:3-6
No true Christian deliberately, knowingly, and habitually practices sin.	No one who abides in Him [who lives and remains in communion with and in obedience to Him-- deliberately, knowingly, and habitually] commits (practices) sin. No one who [habitually] sins has either seen or known Him [recognized, perceived, or understood Him, or has had an experiential acquaintance with Him]. 1Jn 3:6
If I don't conform to God's will, I am a child of the devil. If I don't love my fellow believers, I am a child of the devil.	By this it is made clear who take their nature from God and are His children and who take their nature from the devil and are his children: no one who does not practice righteousness [who does not conform to God's will in purpose, thought, and action] is of God; neither is anyone who does not love his brother (his fellow believer in Christ). 1Jn 3:10
Those who adhere to, trust in, and rely on Jesus can be sure they have eternal life.	I write this to you who believe in (adhere to, trust in, and rely on) the name of the Son of God [in the peculiar services and blessings conferred by Him on men], so that you may know [with settled and absolute knowledge] that you [already] have life, yes, eternal life. 1John 5:13

Perverting grace to allow sinful living is to disown and deny our Lord Jesus. Though God rescued the Israelites from Egypt, He later destroyed those of them who refused to adhere to, trust in and rely on Him. We are reminded that perverting grace to permit disobedience carries the same consequence today. Angels who turned from God, and the cities of Sodom and Gomorrah, also serve as examples to warn us of everlasting fire if we disown Jesus. (See also 1Cor 10:5-12 & Heb 4:11)	4 For certain individuals whose condemnation was written about long ago have secretly slipped in among you. They are ungodly people, who pervert the grace of our God into a license for immorality and deny Jesus Christ our only Sovereign and Lord. 5 Though you already know all this, I want to remind you that the Lord at one time delivered his people out of Egypt, but later destroyed those who did not believe. 6 And the angels who did not keep their positions of authority but abandoned their proper dwelling—these he has kept in darkness, bound with everlasting chains for judgment on the great Day. 7 In a similar way, Sodom and Gomorrah and the surrounding towns gave themselves up to sexual immorality and perversion. They serve as an example of those who suffer the punishment of eternal fire. 8 In the very same way, on the strength of their dreams these ungodly people pollute their own bodies, reject authority and heap abuse on celestial beings. Jude1:4-8 NIV
Save sinners but loath even the clothing polluted by their sinful sensuality.	[Strive to] save others, snatching [them] out of [the] fire; on others take pity [but] with fear, loathing even the garment spotted by the flesh and polluted by their sensuality. Jude 1:23
After backsliding, the church is called to repent again or lose their lampstand.	Remember then from what heights you have fallen. Repent (change the inner man to meet God's will) and do the works you did previously [when first you knew the Lord], or else I will visit you and remove your lampstand from its place, unless you change your mind and repent. Rev 2:5

Christians living in sin who don't wake themselves up and repent, risk their name being erased from the Book of Life.	3 Therefore, remember what you received and heard, and obey it, and repent. If you do not wake up, I will come like a thief, and you will never know at what hour I will come against you. 5 The one who conquers will be dressed like them in white clothing, and I will never erase his name from the book of life, but will declare his name before my Father and before his angels. Rev 3:3,5 NET
Being lukewarm is like standing at the very edge of a cliff, sure to fall off if you died just then, for you would be spit out of Christ's mouth. Yet still alive on the cliff, you are dearly and tenderly loved, and called to repent before it's too late.	15 'I know your deeds, that you are neither cold nor hot. I wish you were either cold or hot! 16 So because you are lukewarm, and neither hot nor cold, I am going to vomit you out of my mouth! 17 Because you say, "I am rich and have acquired great wealth, and need nothing," but do not realize that you are wretched, pitiful, poor, blind, and naked, 19 All those I love, I rebuke and discipline. So be earnest and repent! Rev 3:15-16,19 NET
We will be judged by our deeds, motives, aims, words, etc., the sum of which reflect what we truly believed and whom we truly had faith in.	12I [also] saw the dead, great and small; they stood before the throne, and books were opened. Then another book was opened, which is [the Book] of Life. And the dead were judged (sentenced) by what they had done [their whole way of feeling and acting, their aims and endeavors] in accordance with what was recorded in the books. 13And the sea delivered up the dead who were in it, death and Hades (the state of death or disembodied existence) surrendered the dead in them, and all were tried and their cases determined by what they had done [according to their motives, aims, and works]. Rev 20:12-13
We are repaid according to what our own actions merit. Actions count more than words.	Behold, I am coming soon, and I shall bring My wages and rewards with Me, to repay and render to each one just what his own actions and his own work merit. Rev 22:12

Appendix B

IS HELL A REAL PLACE OR IS IT METAPHORICAL?

It is popular today to dismiss hell as a metaphorical concept—to treat it like a lion without teeth and claws—worthy of little concern.

In contrast, Jesus was *very* concerned about hell. Out of love, that none should perish, He speaks of hell in forty-six different verses in the Bible.[1] Eighteen of those mention the *fire* of hell. These verses are in addition to all the other verses in the Bible where people other than Jesus warn us about hell.

This appendix gathers Scripture on the subject of hell for a convenient reading of the facts. The Scripture shows that hell is clearly revealed in the Bible as a real and horrible place of God's judgment. For example, what sort of 'metaphorical smoke' could darken our real sun and sky like the smoke from hell does in Revelation 9:2?

If hell isn't a real and terrible prison of destruction and pain that is to be avoided at all costs, then nothing Jesus said can be taken seriously and literally. Ironically, it is those who treat His words that way, who will discover first hand how real hell is.

One final note before the Scripture: Since *hell* is a general term in

English, it is helpful to be aware of the more specific biblical terms related to hell as you read these passages. Here is an explanation:[2]

Sheol—Hebrew word meaning 'place of the dead', where departed spirits of both the unrighteous and the righteous went (until the time of Christ's ascension) and where spirits of the unrighteous still go. Sheol was divided into two areas by a great chasm, one area of torment for the unrighteous, and one area of blessing (called Abraham's bosom or paradise) for the righteous. At Christ's ascension, the righteous were gathered to heaven, and any righteous who die since then, go directly to heaven.[3] This leaves only the unrighteous going to Sheol where they will be until the final judgment. After the final judgment, they will be cast into the lake of fire.

Hades—Greek word meaning Sheol.

Abaddon—Hebrew word meaning 'place of destruction'.[4] It is described as the abyss, the final place of the accuser Satan.[5] Abaddon is also referred to as the king of the Abyss.[6]

Tartarus—Greek word in 2Pet 2:4 for the prison where rebellious angels are being kept in pits of gloom awaiting their judgment. Scripture doesn't clarify whether this place is within Sheol. Jude 6 refers to this place as having everlasting chains.[7]

Abyss—bottomless pit where Satan the devil will be imprisoned for 1000 years prior to being released for a short time and then being cast into the lake of fire forever.[8] This pit houses the beast of Rev 11:7 and spews forth much smoke.[9]

Gehenna—Greek term used in the Bible first by Jesus in Mt 5:22. It means a place of torment and punishment for the wicked. The name is derived from the Hebrew "valley of Hinnom" which was once a city garbage dump where fires and worms were always present.[10]

Lake of Fire—the place where death and Hades(also called Sheol) will be thrown after judgment, the second death of those whose names are not written in the book of life.[11]

The Pit—general term referring to the grave, or to Sheol, or to the lower regions, or to the pit of destruction as per usage in the Amplified Bible.

Note: Scripture is listed in the order found in the Bible.

As a result of God's judgment, the wicked go to Sheol.	**32**And the earth opened its mouth and swallowed them and their households and [Korah and] all [his] men and all their possessions. **33**They and all that belonged to them went down alive into Sheol (the place of the dead); and the earth closed upon them, and they perished from among the assembly. Num 16:32-33
God's anger toward sin fuels the fire in Sheol and will ultimately devour the earth.	**21**They have moved Me to jealousy with what is not God; they have angered Me with their idols. So I will move them to jealousy with those who are not a people; I will anger them with a foolish nation. **22**For a fire is kindled by My anger, and it burns to the depths of Sheol, devours the earth with its increase, and sets on fire the foundations of the mountains. Deut 32:21-22
Intense darkness and confusion is described.	The land of sunless gloom as intense darkness, [the land] of the shadow of death, without any order, and where the light is as thick darkness. Job 10:22
The wicked are punished with fire, brimstone and scorching wind.	**5**The Lord tests and proves the [unyieldingly] righteous, but His soul abhors the wicked and him who loves violence. **6**Upon the wicked He will rain quick burning coals or snares; fire, brimstone, and a [dreadful] scorching wind shall be the portion of their cup. Ps 11:5-6
Fear and terror consume those who are desolated in a moment.	**18**[After all] You do set the [wicked] in slippery places; You cast them down to ruin and destruction. **19**How they become a desolation in a moment! They are utterly consumed with terrors! Ps 73:18-19
Adulteress leads to prison chambers of death.	[The loose woman's] house is the way to Sheol (Hades, the place of the dead), going down to the chambers of death. Prov 7:27
No productive purpose in Sheol.	**10**Whatever your hand finds to do, do it with all your might, for there is no work or device or knowledge or wisdom in Sheol (the place of the dead), where you are going. Ecc 9:10

Maggots prey upon dead bodies covered in worms.	9Sheol (Hades, the place of the dead) below is stirred up to meet you at your coming [O tyrant Babylonian rulers]; it stirs up the shades of the dead to greet you--even all the chief ones of the earth; it raises from their thrones [in astonishment at your humbled condition] all the kings of the nations. 10All of them will [tauntingly] say to you, Have you also become weak as we are? Have you become like us? 11Your pomp and magnificence are brought down to Sheol (the underworld), along with the sound of your harps; the maggots [which prey upon dead bodies] are spread out under you and worms cover you [O Babylonian rulers]. Is 14:9-11
Imprisoned, and judged to punishment or pardon.	And they will be gathered together as prisoners are gathered in a pit or dungeon; they will be shut up in prison, and after many days they will be visited, inspected, and punished or pardoned. Is 24:22
Once in Sheol, it's too late to call out to God.	For Sheol (the place of the dead) cannot confess and reach out the hand to You, death cannot praise and rejoice in You; they who go down to the pit cannot hope for Your faithfulness [to Your promises; their probation is at an end, their destiny is sealed]. Is 38:18
Confusion in hell for the wicked contrasted with eternal salvation.	16They shall be put to shame, yes, confounded, all of them; they who are makers of idols shall go off into confusion together. 17But Israel shall be saved by the Lord with an everlasting salvation; you shall not be put to shame or confounded to all eternity. Is 45:16-17
No peace for the wicked.	There is no peace, says my God, for the wicked. Is 57:21
God judges rightly and gives vengeance as is due.	But, O Lord of hosts, Who judges rightly and justly, Who tests the heart and the mind, let me see Your vengeance on them, for to You I have revealed and committed my cause [rolling it upon You]. Jer 11:20

The pit is a *place* of the dead that requires *descending* to.	Then I will thrust you down with those who descend into the pit (the place of the dead) to the people of olden times, and I will make you [Tyre] to dwell in the lower world like the places that were desolate of old, with those who go down to the pit, that you be not inhabited or shed forth your glory and renown in the land of the living. Ezk 26:20
God has no pleasure in the death of the wicked. He calls them to repent.	Say to them, As I live, says the Lord God, I have no pleasure in the death of the wicked, but rather that the wicked turn from his way and live. Turn back, turn back from your evil ways, for why will you die, O house of Israel? Ezk 33:11
All will rise again, some to life and some to *everlasting* contempt.	And many of those who sleep in the dust of the earth shall awake: some to everlasting life and some to shame and everlasting contempt and abhorrence. Dan 12:2
Those who disregard God's relevance will be punished.	And at that time I will search Jerusalem with lamps and punish the men who [like old wine] are thickening and settling on their lees, who say in their hearts, The Lord will not do good, nor will He do evil. Zeph 1:12
Wide is the way that leads to destruction. Few find the narrow way.	13Enter through the narrow gate; for wide is the gate and spacious and broad is the way that leads away to destruction, and many are those who are entering through it. 14But the gate is narrow (contracted by pressure) and the way is straitened and compressed that leads away to life, and few are those who find it. Mt 7:13-14
Our souls are at stake.	And do not be afraid of those who kill the body but cannot kill the soul; but rather be afraid of Him who can destroy both soul and body in hell (Gehenna). Mt 10:28

In keeping with God's justice, the wicked will be cast into fire resulting in weeping and wailing and grinding of teeth—a reasonable response to real fire.	47 "Once again, the kingdom of heaven is like a net that was let down into the lake and caught all kinds of fish. 48 When it was full, the fishermen pulled it up on the shore. Then they sat down and collected the good fish in baskets, but threw the bad away. 49 This is how it will be at the end of the age. The angels will come and separate the wicked from the righteous 50 and throw them into the blazing furnace, where there will be weeping and gnashing of teeth. Mt 13:47-50 NIV
Torture and wrath is in store for those who do not freely forgive.	34And in wrath his master turned him over to the torturers (the jailers), till he should pay all that he owed. 35So also My heavenly Father will deal with every one of you if you do not freely forgive your brother from your heart his offenses. Mt 18:34-35
More weeping and grinding of teeth for the disobedient.	13Then the king said to the attendants, Tie him hand and foot, and throw him into the darkness outside; there will be weeping and grinding of teeth. 14For many are called (invited and summoned), but few are chosen. Mt 22:13-14
Increased degrees of punishment in hell according to what is deserved.	14Woe to you, scribes and Pharisees, pretenders (hypocrites)! For you swallow up widows' houses and for a pretense to cover it up make long prayers; therefore you will receive the greater condemnation and the heavier sentence. 15Woe to you, scribes and Pharisees, pretenders (hypocrites)! For you travel over sea and land to make a single proselyte, and when he becomes one [a proselyte], you make him doubly as much a child of hell (Gehenna) as you are. Mt 23:14-15
The penalty of hell includes *real* suffering.	You serpents! You spawn of vipers! How can you escape the penalty to be suffered in hell (Gehenna)? Mt 23:33
More weeping and grinding of teeth.	And throw the good-for-nothing servant into the outer darkness; there will be weeping and grinding of teeth. Mt 24:30

Punishment is due to pretenders and hypocrites resulting in more weeping and grinding of teeth.	**50**The master of that servant will come on a day when he does not expect him and at an hour of which he is not aware, **51**And will punish him [cut him up by scourging] and put him with the pretenders (hypocrites); there will be weeping and grinding of teeth. Mt 24:50-51
Eternal hell fire was prepared for the devil but will be shared by those who reject Christ.	**41**Then He will say to those at His left hand, Begone from Me, you cursed, into the eternal fire prepared for the devil and his angels! **42**For I was hungry and you gave Me no food, I was thirsty and you gave Me nothing to drink, Mt 25:41-42
Eternal punishment, not one time punishment, is the future of those who reject Christ.	**45**And He will reply to them, Solemnly I declare to you, in so far as you failed to do it for the least [in the estimation of men] of these, you failed to do it for Me. **46**Then they will go away into eternal punishment, but those who are just and upright and in right standing with God into eternal life. Mt 25:45-46
Hell is definitely worse than death by drowning and worse than being maimed and worse than losing an eye. Worms and fire live on in hell.	**42** "But whoever causes one of these little ones who believe in Me to stumble, it would be better for him if a millstone were hung around his neck, and he were thrown into the sea. **43** If your hand causes you to sin, cut it off. It is better for you to enter into life maimed, rather than having two hands, to go to hell, into the fire that shall never be quenched— **44** where 'Their worm does not die And the fire is not quenched.' **45** And if your foot causes you to sin, cut it off. It is better for you to enter life lame, rather than having two feet, to be cast into hell, into the fire that shall never be quenched— **46** where 'Their worm does not die, And the fire is not quenched.' **47** And if your eye causes you to sin, pluck it out. It is better for you to enter the kingdom of God with one eye, rather than having two eyes, to be cast into hell fire— **48** where 'Their worm does not die And the fire is not quenched.' Mark 9:42-48 NKJV

He who doesn't adhere to and rely on Christ is condemned to eternal death.	He who believes [who adheres to and trusts in and relies on the Gospel and Him Whom it sets forth] and is baptized will be saved [from the penalty of eternal death]; but he who does not believe [who does not adhere to and trust in and rely on the Gospel and Him Whom it sets forth] will be condemned. Mark 16:16
Various degrees of punishment are given depending on what amount of knowledge a person is accountable for receiving.	45 But suppose the servant says to himself, 'My master is taking a long time in coming,' and he then begins to beat the other servants, both men and women, and to eat and drink and get drunk. 46 The master of that servant will come on a day when he does not expect him and at an hour he is not aware of. He will cut him to pieces and assign him a place with the unbelievers. 47 "The servant who knows the master's will and does not get ready or does not do what the master wants will be beaten with many blows. 48 But the one who does not know and does things deserving punishment will be beaten with few blows. From everyone who has been given much, much will be demanded; and from the one who has been entrusted with much, much more will be asked. Lk 12:45-48 NIV
Repent or perish eternally.	I tell you, No; but unless you repent (change your mind for the better and heartily amend your ways, with abhorrence of your past sins), you will all likewise perish and be lost eternally. Lk 13:3

The heat of flames draws excruciating thirst—a reasonable response to *real* heat and flames. Anguish, or else comfort and delights, is our choice. Once the choice is sealed by dying, there is no reversing it. Even the man already receiving the punishment is concerned for his unsaved brothers, hoping to avert their same disaster.	**23** In Hades, where he was in torment, he looked up and saw Abraham far away, with Lazarus by his side. **24** So he called to him, 'Father Abraham, have pity on me and send Lazarus to dip the tip of his finger in water and cool my tongue, because I am in agony in this fire.' **25** "But Abraham replied, 'Son, remember that in your lifetime you received your good things, while Lazarus received bad things, but now he is comforted here and you are in agony. **26** And besides all this, between us and you a great chasm has been set in place, so that those who want to go from here to you cannot, nor can anyone cross over from there to us.' **27** "He answered, 'Then I beg you, father, send Lazarus to my family, **28** for I have five brothers. Let him warn them, so that they will not also come to this place of torment.' **29** "Abraham replied, 'They have Moses and the Prophets; let them listen to them.' **30** "'No, father Abraham,' he said, 'but if someone from the dead goes to them, they will repent.' **31** "He said to him, 'If they do not listen to Moses and the Prophets, they will not be convinced even if someone rises from the dead.'" Lk 16:23-31 NIV
Remain in Christ or be thrown into the fire.	If a person does not dwell in Me, he is thrown out like a [broken-off] branch, and withers; such branches are gathered up and thrown into the fire, and they are burned. John 15:6
In the end, all will bow the knee to Christ and each will give an account of himself.	**11** For it is written, As I live, says the Lord, every knee shall bow to Me, and every tongue shall confess to God [acknowledge Him to His honor and to His praise]. **12** And so each of us shall give an account of himself [give an answer in reference to judgment] to God. Rom 14:11-12

God's Kingdom will not receive entry of wrongdoers.	9Do you not know that the unrighteous and the wrongdoers will not inherit or have any share in the kingdom of God? Do not be deceived (misled): neither the impure and immoral, nor idolaters, nor adulterers, nor those who participate in homosexuality, 10Nor cheats (swindlers and thieves), nor greedy graspers, nor drunkards, nor foulmouthed revilers and slanderers, nor extortioners and robbers will inherit or have any share in the kingdom of God. 1Cor 6:9-10
People who distress and afflict God's people get distress and affliction from God in return. Suffering and punishment of everlasting ruin goes to those who refuse to obey the Gospel of Christ.	6 God is just: He will pay back trouble to those who trouble you 7 and give relief to you who are troubled, and to us as well. This will happen when the Lord Jesus is revealed from heaven in blazing fire with his powerful angels. 8 He will punish those who do not know God and do not obey the gospel of our Lord Jesus. 9 They will be punished with everlasting destruction and shut out from the presence of the Lord and from the glory of his might 2Thes 1:6-9 NIV
Everyone dies and is judged.	And just as it is appointed for [all] men once to die, and after that the [certain] judgment, Heb 9:27
A greater level of punishment is given to those who have known Christ and then rejected Him.	26 If we deliberately keep on sinning after we have received the knowledge of the truth, no sacrifice for sins is left, 27 but only a fearful expectation of judgment and of raging fire that will consume the enemies of God. 28 Anyone who rejected the law of Moses died without mercy on the testimony of two or three witnesses. 29 How much more severely do you think someone deserves to be punished who has trampled the Son of God underfoot, who has treated as an unholy thing the blood of the covenant that sanctified them, and who has insulted the Spirit of grace? 30 For we know him who said, "It is mine to avenge; I will repay," and again, "The Lord will judge his people." 31 It is a dreadful thing to fall into the hands of the living God. Heb 10:26-31 NIV

God will judge everyone.	But they will have to give an account to Him Who is ready to judge and pass sentence on the living and the dead. 1Pet 4:5
Ungodly are chastised until the day of judgment and doom. They are destined for punishment as a reward for their disobedience.	9Now if [all these things are true, then be sure] the Lord knows how to rescue the godly out of temptations and trials, and how to keep the ungodly under chastisement until the day of judgment and doom, 10And particularly those who walk after the flesh and indulge in the lust of polluting passion and scorn and despise authority. Presumptuous [and] daring [self-willed and self-loving creatures]! 12But these [people]! Like unreasoning beasts, mere creatures of instinct, born [only] to be captured and destroyed, railing at things of which they are ignorant, they shall utterly perish in their [own] corruption [in their destroying they shall surely be destroyed], 13Being destined to receive [punishment as] the reward of [their] unrighteousness [suffering wrong as the hire for their wrongdoing]. They count it a delight to revel in the daytime [living luxuriously and delicately]. They are blots and blemishes, reveling in their deceptions and carousing together [even] as they feast with you. 2Pet 2:9-10, 12-13
God desires no one to perish but that all would repent.	The Lord does not delay and is not tardy or slow about what He promises, according to some people's conception of slowness, but He is long-suffering (extraordinarily patient) toward you, not desiring that any should perish, but that all should turn to repentance. 2Pet 3:9
Fallen angels are in prison and in eternal chains in darkness, waiting for judgment day.	And angels who did not keep (care for, guard, and hold to) their own first place of power but abandoned their proper dwelling place--these He has reserved in custody in eternal chains (bonds) under the thick gloom of utter darkness until the judgment and doom of the great day. Jude 6

Earth's *real* sky is darkened by hell's *real* smoke. Metaphorical smoke wouldn't darken our real sky.	He opened the long shaft of the Abyss (the bottomless pit), and smoke like the smoke of a huge furnace puffed out of the long shaft, so that the sun and the atmosphere were darkened by the smoke from the long shaft. Rev 9:2
Abyss is a bottomless pit of destruction.	Over them as king they have the angel of the Abyss (of the bottomless pit). In Hebrew his name is Abaddon [destruction], but in Greek he is called Apollyon [destroyer]. Rev 9:11
God's undiluted indignation and wrath brings torment with fire and brimstone forever and ever without pause or rest or intermission or peace, day or night, to those who receive the mark of the beast or show him respect.	9Then another angel, a third, followed them, saying with a mighty voice, Whoever pays homage to the beast and his statue and permits the [beast's] stamp (mark, inscription) to be put on his forehead or on his hand, 10He too shall [have to] drink of the wine of God's indignation and wrath, poured undiluted into the cup of His anger; and he shall be tormented with fire and brimstone in the presence of the angels and in the presence of the Lamb. 11And the smoke of their torment ascends forever and ever; and they have no respite (no pause, no intermission, no rest, no peace) day or night-- these who pay homage to the beast and to his image and whoever receives the stamp of his name upon him. Rev 14:9-11

Torment day and night in the fiery lake of burning brimstone is in store for the devil and all whose names are not found in the Book of Life. This is called the second death. We are all judged by what we have done (our motives, aims, and works).	10Then the devil who had led them astray [deceiving and seducing them] was hurled into the fiery lake of burning brimstone, where the beast and false prophet were; and they will be tormented day and night forever and ever (through the ages of the ages). 11Then I saw a great white throne and the One Who was seated upon it, from Whose presence and from the sight of Whose face earth and sky fled away, and no place was found for them. 12I [also] saw the dead, great and small; they stood before the throne, and books were opened. Then another book was opened, which is [the Book] of Life. And the dead were judged (sentenced) by what they had done [their whole way of feeling and acting, their aims and endeavors] in accordance with what was recorded in the books. 13And the sea delivered up the dead who were in it, death and Hades (the state of death or disembodied existence) surrendered the dead in them, and all were tried and their cases determined by what they had done [according to their motives, aims, and works]. 14Then death and Hades (the state of death or disembodied existence) were thrown into the lake of fire. This is the second death, the lake of fire. 15And if anyone's [name] was not found recorded in the Book of Life, he was hurled into the lake of fire. Rev 20:10-15

Even cowards and those lacking courage to follow Jesus receive their part in the lake of fire, the second death.	But as for the cowards and the ignoble and the contemptible and the cravenly lacking in courage and the cowardly submissive, and as for the unbelieving and faithless, and as for the depraved and defiled with abominations, and as for murderers and the lewd and adulterous and the practicers of magic arts and the idolaters (those who give supreme devotion to anyone or anything other than God) and all liars (those who knowingly convey untruth by word or deed)--[all of these shall have] their part in the lake that blazes with fire and brimstone. This is the second death. Rev 21:8

The reality of hell is described in the Bible, but God has also graciously seen fit to warn us of hell's reality in another way. He has given numerous people visions of hell, where it is as if they were there in person to experience the pain, the unimaginable fear, the vicious God-hating demons, the thirst, the lack of air, the fire, the loneliness, the stench, the toxic sulfur, the screams, the confusion and the eternal hopelessness of never getting out.

I recommend one such vision available on YouTube and in book form called, *23 Minutes in Hell* by Bill Wiese. Warning: This vision is not for the faint of heart.

Aside from all the descriptions and warnings about hell in the Bible, there is also a strong logical evidence of hell that has to do with God's character. As much as God is love, He is also *just* and *fair*. If He is a *just Judge,* then He must ensure that justice is done, so it follows He would have a place of prison and punishment for the unrepentant. How could a *just Judge* allow sinners to get off scot-free?

Then some people might ask, "But why a *never-ending* prison sentence?" As sinners, we each have a death penalty to pay. By God's infinitely righteous standard, our debt is infinite. Through their disobedience, those who reject Christ's infinitely perfect blood as their payment for sin, must pay for themselves their infinite debt by an infinitely long death penalty.

Again, our infinite death penalty will either be paid by infinitely perfect blood, or by an infinitely long and tortuous prison term. Praise God we've been given a merciful option that we don't deserve!

1. Wiese, Bill. *"23 Minutes in Hell."* Charisma House. 2010. YouTube. 20 Oct 2011. <www.youtube.com/watch?v=NjjBRfvKXa4>
2. Erwin W. Lutzer, *One Minute After You Die* (Chicago: Moody, 1997), 110-111.
3. Eph 4:8-10, Phil 1:21-23, 2Cor 5:8
4. Prov 27:20 (AMP)
5. Prov 15:11 (AMP)
6. Rev 9:11 (AMP)
7. Stewart, Don. "What is Tartarus?" Blueletter Bible FAQs. Post date unknown. 20 Oct. 2011. <www.blueletterbible.org/faq/don_stewart/stewart.cfm?id=167>
8. Rev 20:3,7
9. Rev 9:2
10. Erwin W. Lutzer, One Minute After You Die (Chicago: Moody, 1997), 110-111.
11. Rev 20:14, 21:8

Appendix C

SCRIPTURE THAT REVEALS TRUE ETERNAL SECURITY, AND EXPOSES FALSE ETERNAL SECURITY

C hristians can live in the absolute security of knowing they will be with Christ eternally, *if* they choose to *endure* with Christ. This is true eternal security. However, there is also a *false* eternal security often taught. It guarantees a person salvation on the basis of a *salvation event in their past*, no matter how they live. It leaves people assured that once they're in, they're in! They don't realize the crucial role that repentance and obedience has in *obtaining* and *retaining* salvation in Christ, and they ignore what God says about those who don't *endure*.

"Therefore, dear friends, since you have been forewarned, be on your guard so that you may not be carried away by the error of the lawless and *fall from your secure position*" (2Pet 3:17, NIV, emphasis mine).

The following passages contrast sharply with the idea that Christians can live lifestyles of sin and expect to retain their salvation. They remind us that there is a very important "if...then" aspect to eternal security.

Note: Scripture is listed in the order found in the Bible.

God is faithful and will never forsake or abandon those who follow Him, but those who forsake or reject Him and break His covenant with them can expect to be forsaken by Him if they don't repent.	**6** Be strong and courageous! Do not fear or tremble before them, for the Lord your God is the one who is going with you. He will not fail you or abandon you!" **16** Then the Lord said to Moses, "You are about to die, and then these people will begin to prostitute themselves with the foreign gods of the land into which they are going. They will reject me and break my covenant that I have made with them. **17** At that time my anger will erupt against them and I will abandon them and hide my face from them until they are devoured. Many disasters and distresses will overcome them so that they will say at that time, 'Have not these disasters overcome us because our God is not among us?' Deut 31:6, 16, 17 NET
Some people use the passage about the prodigal son to suggest "once a son, always a son" in order to prove "once saved, always saved." In actual fact, we can lose our sonship. Deuteronomy 32 makes it clear that the children of God (the Israelites) were mistaken to believe they were still sons of God. Instead He says they are corrupt and not his children.	They are corrupt and not his children; to their shame they are a warped and crooked generation. Deut 32:5 NIV

154

Obedience results in blessing. Disobedience results in the blessing being revoked.	**4** You must serve me with integrity and sincerity, just as your father David did. Do everything I commanded and obey my rules and regulations. **5** Then I will allow your dynasty to rule over Israel permanently, just as I promised your father David, 'You will not fail to have a successor on the throne of Israel.' **6** "But if you or your sons ever turn away from me, fail to obey the regulations and rules I instructed you to keep, and decide to serve and worship other gods, **7** then I will remove Israel from the land I have given them, I will abandon this temple I have consecrated with my presence, and Israel will be mocked and ridiculed among all the nations. 1 Kings 9:4-7 NET
Solomon's kingdom will last forever *if* he will continuously obey God. If instead, he forsakes God, God will cast him off *forever.*	**7** I will establish his kingdom permanently, if he remains committed to obeying my commands and regulations, as you are doing this day.' **8** So now, in the sight of all Israel, the Lord's assembly, and in the hearing of our God, I say this: Carefully observe all the commands of the Lord your God, so that you may possess this good land and may leave it as a permanent inheritance for your children after you. **9** "And you, Solomon my son, obey the God of your father and serve him with a submissive attitude and a willing spirit, for the Lord examines all minds and understands every motive of one's thoughts. If you seek him, he will let you find him, but if you abandon him, he will reject you permanently. 1Chr 28:7, 9 NET

After serving the Lord faithfully, Joash later forsakes God. God seeks to draw Joash back, but when Joash insists on forsaking the Lord, eventually the Lord forsakes Joash. Forsake God and eventually He will forsake you.	**2** Joash did what the Lord approved throughout the lifetime of Jehoiada the priest. **17** After Jehoiada died, the officials of Judah visited the king and declared their loyalty to him. The king listened to their advice. **18** They abandoned the temple of the Lord God of their ancestors, and worshiped the Asherah poles and idols. Because of this sinful activity, God was angry with Judah and Jerusalem. **19** The Lord sent prophets among them to lead them back to him. They warned the people, but they would not pay attention. **20** God's Spirit energized Zechariah son of Jehoiada the priest. He stood up before the people and said to them, "This is what God says: 'Why are you violating the commands of the Lord? You will not be prosperous! Because you have rejected the Lord, he has rejected you!'" 2Chronicles 24:2 & 17-20 NET
Solomon walked close to God and God loved him, but when he was old he turned treacherously away from God to serve other gods.	Did not Solomon king of Israel act treacherously against God and miss the mark on account of such women? Among many nations there was no king like him. He was loved by his God, and God made him king over all Israel; yet strange women even caused him to sin [when he was old he turned treacherously away from the Lord to other gods, and God rent his kingdom from him]. Neh 13:26
According to David's very real concern, the presence of God and specifically the Holy Spirit can be removed from those He was once with.	Cast me not away from Your presence and take not Your Holy Spirit from me. Ps 51:11
The possibility of names being removed from the book of life is consistent with the rest of Scripture. (See Rev 17:8 and Rev 3:5)	Let them be blotted out of the book of the living and the book of life and not be enrolled among the [uncompromisingly] righteous (those upright and in right standing with God). Ps 69:28

Those who depart from God are destroyed.	For behold, those who are far from You shall perish; You will destroy all who are false to You and like [spiritual] harlots depart from You. Ps 73:27
He was *in* the way of understanding but wandered *out*. His destiny is death.	A man who wanders out of the way of understanding shall abide in the congregation of the spirits (of the dead). Prov 21:16
Here, after much patience, God forsakes His beloved children into their enemies' hands since they abandoned Him.	I have forsaken My house, I have cast off My heritage; I have given the dearly beloved of My life into the hands of her enemies. Jer 12:7
If a righteous man *turns from his righteousness* and does evil, he will *die* for it. If an evil man *turns from His evil* and obeys God, he will inherit *life*. This is repeated three times in this passage alone.	**12** "And you, son of man, say to your people, 'The righteousness of the righteous will not deliver him if he rebels. As for the wicked, his wickedness will not make him stumble if he turns from it. The righteous will not be able to live by his righteousness if he sins.' **13** Suppose I tell the righteous that he will certainly live, but he becomes confident in his righteousness and commits iniquity. None of his righteous deeds will be remembered; because of the iniquity he has committed he will die. **14** Suppose I say to the wicked, 'You must certainly die,' but he turns from his sin and does what is just and right. **15** He returns what was taken in pledge, pays back what he has stolen, and follows the statutes that give life, committing no iniquity. He will certainly live – he will not die. **16** None of the sins he has committed will be counted against him. He has done what is just and right; he will certainly live. **17** "Yet your people say, 'The behavior of the Lord is not right,' when it is their behavior that is not right. **18** When a righteous man turns from his godliness and commits iniquity, he will die for it. **19** When the wicked turns from his sin and does what is just and right, he will live because of it. Ezk 33:12-19 NET

With whom does God keep His covenant of mercy and loving-kindness? "With those who love Him and keep His commandments."	4And I prayed to the Lord my God and made confession and said, O Lord, the great and dreadful God, Who keeps covenant, mercy, and loving-kindness with those who love Him and keep His commandments 14Therefore the Lord has kept ready the calamity (evil) and has brought it upon us, for the Lord our God is [uncompromisingly] righteous and rigidly just in all His works which He does [keeping His word]; and we have not obeyed His voice. Daniel 9:4, 14
Reject God long enough and eventually He'll reject you.	6My people are destroyed for lack of knowledge; because you [the priestly nation] have rejected knowledge, I will also reject you that you shall be no priest to Me; seeing you have forgotten the law of your God, I will also forget your children. 7The more they increased and multiplied [in prosperity and power], the more they sinned against Me; I will change their glory into shame. Hosea 4:6-7
God is patient and first seeks to draw people back to Himself, but eventually He *cuts off* those who draw back from following Him.	4 "I will attack Judah and all who live in Jerusalem. I will remove from this place every trace of Baal worship, as well as the very memory of the pagan priests. 5 I will remove those who worship the stars in the sky from their rooftops, those who swear allegiance to the Lord while taking oaths in the name of their 'king,' 6 and those who turn their backs on the Lord and do not want the Lord's help or guidance." Zeph 1:4-6 NET
Endurance is required to secure salvation. No one can rest assured on a one-time salvation event if they are not persevering.	And you will be hated by all for My name's sake, but he who perseveres and endures to the end will be saved [from spiritual disease and death in the world to come]. Mt 10:22

Here a person hears the salvation message, accepts it, but endures only until persecution comes. Then he falls away.	20As for what was sown on thin (rocky) soil, this is he who hears the Word and at once welcomes and accepts it with joy; 21Yet it has no real root in him, but is temporary (inconstant, lasts but a little while); and when affliction or trouble or persecution comes on account of the Word, at once he is caused to stumble [he is repelled and begins to distrust and desert Him Whom he ought to trust and obey] and he falls away. Mt 13:20-21
Jesus warns His own disciples to be careful not to be led astray. In other words, it's possible for true believers to be led astray.	4Jesus answered them, Be careful that no one misleads you [deceiving you and leading you into error]. 5For many will come in (on the strength of) My name [appropriating the name which belongs to Me], saying, I am the Christ (the Messiah), and they will lead many astray. Mt 24:4-5
To "begin to distrust" Christ, means there had been a trust in the past. This one-time trust did not change the fact that later, these people deserted Christ, fell away and hated each other instead of loving each other.	And then many will be offended and repelled and will begin to distrust and desert [Him Whom they ought to trust and obey] and will stumble and fall away and betray one another and pursue one another with hatred. Mt 24:10
Endurance is required to secure salvation. No one can rest assured on a one-time salvation event if he is not persevering.	11And many false prophets will rise up and deceive and lead many into error. 12And the love of the great body of people will grow cold because of the multiplied lawlessness and iniquity, 13But he who endures to the end will be saved. Mt 24:11-13

Jesus teaches about people who believe but later fall away.	And those upon the rock [are the people] who, when they hear [the Word], receive and welcome it with joy; but these have no root. They believe for a while, and in time of trial and temptation fall away (withdraw and stand aloof). Luke 8:13
An unfaithful servant will be punished, cut off, and assigned to be with the unfaithful.	The master of that servant will come on a day when he does not expect him and at an hour of which he does not know, and will punish him and cut him off and assign his lot with the unfaithful. Lk 12:46
Dwelling in Jesus requires obeying Him and enduring. If we keep His commandments we stay on in His love. If we don't, we are broken off Him and thrown into the fire.	4 Remain in me, and I will remain in you. Just as the branch cannot bear fruit by itself, unless it remains in the vine, so neither can you unless you remain in me. 5 "I am the vine; you are the branches. The one who remains in me – and I in him – bears much fruit, because apart from me you can accomplish nothing. 6 If anyone does not remain in me, he is thrown out like a branch, and dries up; and such branches are gathered up and thrown into the fire, and are burned up. 10 If you obey my commandments, you will remain in my love, just as I have obeyed my Father's commandments and remain in his love. John 15:4-6, 10 NET
Judas was not only a disciple, but an *apostle* of Christ, yet he turned astray and perished.	17 For he [Judas] was counted among us and received [by divine allotment] his portion in this ministry. 25 To take the place in this ministry and receive the position of an apostle, from which Judas fell away and went astray to go [where he belonged] to his own [proper] place. Acts 1:17 & 25

Believers are warned here that if they turn and again follow the sinful nature, they will surely die. Alternatively, if they continually follow God, they will certainly live forever. We are secure knowing God is faithful to His words.	For if you live according to [the dictates of] the flesh, you will surely die. But if through the power of the [Holy] Spirit you are [habitually] putting to death (making extinct, deadening) the [evil] deeds prompted by the body, you shall [really and genuinely] live forever. Rom 8:13
God's Holy Spirit gives witness inside a true child of God assuring he is indeed a child of God. (See also Eph 1:3, 2Cor 1:22 and 1Jn 3:24)	The Spirit Himself [thus] testifies together with our own spirit, [assuring us] that we are children of God. Rom 8:16
Although a Gentile Christian has been grafted into Christ, he won't be spared if he becomes proud and conceited and unbelieving. He will be pruned off just like the natural branches of Israel were when they became proud and unbelieving.	17 But if some of the branches were broken off, while you, a wild olive shoot, were grafted in among them to share the richness [of the root and sap] of the olive tree, 18 Do not boast over the branches and pride yourself at their expense. If you do boast and feel superior, remember it is not you that support the root, but the root [that supports] you. 19 You will say then, Branches were broken (pruned) off so that I might be grafted in! 20 That is true. But they were broken (pruned) off because of their unbelief (their lack of real faith), and you are established through faith [because you do believe]. So do not become proud and conceited, but rather stand in awe and be reverently afraid. 21 For if God did not spare the natural branches [because of unbelief], neither will He spare you [if you are guilty of the same offense]. Rom 11:17-21

God's grace and kindness is for those who *continue* and *abide* in it. This endurance is a choice, just like initial repentance is a choice. Being cut off is the alternative to enduring.	Then note and appreciate the gracious kindness and the severity of God: severity toward those who have fallen, but God's gracious kindness to you-- provided you continue in His grace and abide in His kindness; otherwise you too will be cut off (pruned away). Rom 11:22
Even Paul realizes he could walk away from salvation and be rejected if he didn't choose to persevere.	But [like a boxer] I buffet my body [handle it roughly, discipline it by hardships] and subdue it, for fear that after proclaiming to others the Gospel and things pertaining to it, I myself should become unfit [not stand the test, be unapproved and rejected as a counterfeit]. 1Cor 9:27
Although God had saved His children Israel out of Egypt, the death that disobedient Israel earned in the wilderness serves to warn us against disobedience after we've been saved today. If we choose disobedience, we can expect the same result they got—death. Sin is still just as venomous and serious to God on this side of the cross as it was on the other side of the cross. (See also Heb 4:11 & Jude 1:4-8)	**5** But God was not pleased with most of them, for they were cut down in the wilderness. **6** These things happened as examples for us, so that we will not crave evil things as they did. **7** So do not be idolaters, as some of them were. As it is written, *"The people sat down to eat and drink and rose up to play."* **8** And let us not be immoral, as some of them were, and twenty-three thousand died in a single day. **9** And let us not put Christ to the test, as some of them did, and were destroyed by snakes. **10** And do not complain, as some of them did, and were killed by the destroying angel. **11** These things happened to them as examples and were written for our instruction, on whom the ends of the ages have come. **12** So let the one who thinks he is standing be careful that he does not fall. 1Cor 10:5-12 NET

Endurance is required to secure salvation. No one can rest assured on a one-time salvation event if he is not persevering.	1AND NOW let me remind you [since it seems to have escaped you], brethren, of the Gospel (the glad tidings of salvation) which I proclaimed to you, which you welcomed and accepted and upon which your faith rests, 2And by which you are saved, if you hold fast and keep firmly what I preached to you, unless you believed at first without effect and all for nothing. 1Cor 15:1-2
True eternal security (for the repentant) comes from knowing God is faithful to keep His promises. God has even given true believers the Holy Spirit as a seal and a security deposit to assure us. (See also Eph 1:13, 1Jn 3:24 and Rom 8:16)	[He has also appropriated and acknowledged us as His by] putting His seal upon us and giving us His [Holy] Spirit in our hearts as the security deposit and guarantee [of the fulfillment of His promise]. 2Cor 1:22
Those who have had a wholehearted and *sincere and pure devotion to Christ* can be corrupted and seduced if they go after another Jesus, or a different spirit, or a different gospel.	3But [now] I am fearful, lest that even as the serpent beguiled Eve by his cunning, so your minds may be corrupted and seduced from wholehearted and sincere and pure devotion to Christ. 4For [you seem readily to endure it] if a man comes and preaches another Jesus than the One we preached, or if you receive a different spirit from the [Spirit] you [once] received or a different gospel from the one you [then] received and welcomed; you tolerate [all that] well enough! 2Corinthians 11:3-4
Believers can sever themselves from Christ and fall away by relying on the keeping of the Law for justification.	If you seek to be justified and declared righteous and to be given a right standing with God through the Law, you are brought to nothing and so separated (severed) from Christ. You have fallen away from grace (from God's gracious favor and unmerited blessing). Gal 5:4

True eternal security (for those who believe, adhere to and rely on Jesus) is further assured by the giving of the Holy Spirit. (See also 2Cor 1:22, 1Jn 3:24 and Rom 8:16)	In Him you also who have heard the Word of Truth, the glad tidings (Gospel) of your salvation, and have believed in and adhered to and relied on Him, were stamped with the seal of the long-promised Holy Spirit. Eph 1:13
Our salvation hinges on an important "if"—if we continue in the faith.	21 Once you were alienated from God and were enemies in your minds because of your evil behavior. 22 But now he has reconciled you by Christ's physical body through death to present you holy in his sight, without blemish and free from accusation— 23 if you continue in your faith, established and firm, and do not move from the hope held out in the gospel. This is the gospel that you heard and that has been proclaimed to every creature under heaven, and of which I, Paul, have become a servant. Col 1:21-23 NIV
Paul is concerned that his converts are *enduring* in their faith or his work would have been fruitless.	That is the reason that, when I could bear [the suspense] no longer, I sent that I might learn [how you were standing the strain, and the endurance of] your faith, [for I was fearful] lest somehow the tempter had tempted you and our toil [among you should prove to] be fruitless and to no purpose. 1Thes 3:5
Apostasy is a falling away of people who have professed Christ.	Let no one deceive or beguile you in any way, for that day will not come except the apostasy comes first [unless the predicted great falling away of those who have professed to be Christians has come], and the man of lawlessness (sin) is revealed, who is the son of doom (of perdition), 2Thes 2:3

A shipwrecked faith can be salvaged through discipline. It may also go the other way if repentance does not occur.	19By rejecting and thrusting from them [their conscience], some individuals have made shipwreck of their faith. 20Among them are Hymenaeus and Alexander, whom I have delivered to Satan in order that they may be disciplined [by punishment and learn] not to blaspheme. 1Tim 1:19b-20
A believer who is a recent convert should not be chosen as an elder, or conceit could develop and he could fall and come under the same judgment as the devil!	He must not be a recent convert, or he may become conceited and fall under the same judgment as the devil. 1Tim 3:6
Turning from faith in God remains an option.	BUT THE [Holy] Spirit distinctly and expressly declares that in latter times some will turn away from the faith, giving attention to deluding and seducing spirits and doctrines that demons teach, 1Tim 4:1
People of faith have turned away from God to Satan.	For already some [widows] have turned aside after Satan. 1Tim 5:15
The love of money can cause people to wander from the faith.	For the love of money is a root of all evils; it is through this craving that some have been led astray and have wandered from the faith and pierced themselves through with many acute [mental] pangs. 1Tim 6:10
If we endure, all is good. If we don't, He will deny, disown and reject us.	If we endure, we shall also reign with Him. If we deny and disown and reject Him, He will also deny and disown and reject us. 2Tim 2:12

Not only did these people depart from the truth but they destroyed the faith of others too.	**17** Their teaching will spread like gangrene. Among them are Hymenaeus and Philetus, **18** who have departed from the truth. They say that the resurrection has already taken place, and they destroy the faith of some. 2Tim 2:17-18
Endurance is required to secure salvation. No one can rest assured on a one-time salvation event if he is not persevering.	But Christ (the Messiah) was faithful over His [own Father's] house as a Son [and Master of it]. And it is we who are [now members] of this house, if we hold fast and firm to the end our joyful and exultant confidence and sense of triumph in our hope [in Christ]. Heb 3:6
It is possible for a believer to become unbelieving, (refusing to cleave to, trust in, and rely on Jesus), to turn away and to desert God. We are warned to be careful this doesn't happen to us.	[Therefore beware] brethren, take care, lest there be in any one of you a wicked, unbelieving heart [which refuses to cleave to, trust in, and rely on Him], leading you to turn away and desert or stand aloof from the living God. Heb 3:12
Endurance is required to secure salvation. No one can rest assured on a one-time salvation event if he is not persevering.	For we have become fellows with Christ (the Messiah) and share in all He has for us, if only we hold our first newborn confidence and original assured expectation [in virtue of which we are believers] firm and unshaken to the end. Heb 3:14

Enduring obedience takes diligent effort. It is as crucial today as it was in Moses' day. Disobedience has similar consequences today as it did then. (See also 1Cor 10:5-12 & Jude 1:4-8)	Let us therefore be zealous and exert ourselves and strive diligently to enter that rest [of God, to know and experience it for ourselves], that no one may fall or perish by the same kind of unbelief and disobedience [into which those in the wilderness fell]. Heb 4:11
Christians (people who have repented, been enlightened, and shared the Holy Spirit) who later not only sin, but actually turn away from their allegiance to Christ, cannot be brought back to repentance. (See also 1Jn 5:16)	4For it is impossible [to restore and bring again to repentance] those who have been once for all enlightened, who have consciously tasted the heavenly gift and have become sharers of the Holy Spirit, 5And have felt how good the Word of God is and the mighty powers of the age and world to come, 6If they then deviate from the faith and turn away from their allegiance--[it is impossible] to bring them back to repentance, for (because, while, as long as) they nail upon the cross the Son of God afresh [as far as they are concerned] and are holding [Him] up to contempt and shame and public disgrace. Heb 6:4-6

Believers who go on willingly sinning without repentance have no hope but to look forward to God's judgment and burning wrath. Their punishment will be worse than those who didn't follow Moses, because they have trampled underfoot the Son of God. It's a terrible thing to incur such a penalty from God. It would be far better to repent!	26 For if we deliberately keep on sinning after receiving the knowledge of the truth, no further sacrifice for sins is left for us, 27 but only a certain fearful expectation of judgment and *a fury of fire that will consume God's enemies.* 28 Someone who rejected the law of Moses was put to death without mercy *on the testimony of two or three witnesses.* 29 How much greater punishment do you think that person deserves who has contempt for the Son of God, and profanes the blood of the covenant that made him holy, and insults the Spirit of grace? 30 For we know the one who said, *"Vengeance is mine, I will repay,"* and again, *"The Lord will judge his people."* 31 It is a terrifying thing to fall into the hands of the living God. 39 But we are not among those who shrink back and thus perish, but are among those who have faith and preserve their souls. Heb 10:26-31, 39 NET
The Lord promises the crown of life to those who love Him. But there is a condition. Endurance. (See Rev 2:10 and Rev 3:11)	Blessed *is* the man who *endures temptation; for when he has been approved,* he will receive the crown of life which the Lord has promised to those who love Him. James 1:12, NKJV
Speaking of *Christian brothers*, one brother's *soul is saved from death* by the other who turns him back from his sin.	19[My] brethren, if anyone among you strays from the Truth and falls into error and another [person] brings him back [to God], 20Let the [latter] one be sure that whoever turns a sinner from his evil course will save [that one's] soul from death and will cover a multitude of sins [procure the pardon of the many sins committed by the convert]. James 5:19-20

An unbeliever is better off than a person who once walked with Jesus, but later is entangled *and overcome* again with sin. Essentially, this person has repented of his repentance, returning again to his first condition, except worse.	**20** For if after they have escaped the filthy things of the world through the rich knowledge of our Lord and Savior Jesus Christ, they again get entangled in them and succumb to them, their last state has become worse for them than their first. **21** For it would have been better for them never to have known the way of righteousness than, having known it, to turn back from the holy commandment that had been delivered to them. **22** They are illustrations of this true proverb: "*A dog returns to its own vomit*," and "A sow, after washing herself, wallows in the mire." 2Pet 2:20-22 NET
Christians are warned to watch out that they don't *fall* from their *secure position.*	Therefore, dear friends, since you have been forewarned, be on your guard so that you may not be carried away by the error of the lawless and fall from your secure position. 2Pet 3:17 (NIV)
Those who do righteously, conforming to God's will, can be *sure* they are born again.	If you know (perceive and are sure) that He [Christ] is [absolutely] righteous [conforming to the Father's will in purpose, thought, and action], you may also know (be sure) that everyone who does righteously [and is therefore in like manner conformed to the divine will] is born (begotten) of Him [God]. 1Jn 2:29
If we live in obedience to Christ, we know we are saved. And *if* the Holy Spirit lives in us, we have further proof we are saved. (See also Eph 1:3, 2Cor 1:22 and Rom 8:16)	All who keep His commandments [who obey His orders and follow His plan, live and continue to live, to stay and] abide in Him, and He in them. [They let Christ be a home to them and they are the home of Christ.] And by this we know and understand and have the proof that He [really] lives and makes His home in us: by the [Holy] Spirit Whom He has given us. 1Jn 3:24

A person who adheres to, trusts in, and relies on Jesus, can know with secure and settled and absolute knowledge that he is saved into eternal life. This person has an inner witness to this fact.	**10**He who believes in the Son of God [who adheres to, trusts in, and relies on Him] has the testimony [possesses this divine attestation] within himself. He who does not believe God [in this way] has made Him out to be and represented Him as a liar, because he has not believed (put his faith in, adhered to, and relied on) the evidence (the testimony) that God has borne regarding His Son. **11**And this is that testimony (that evidence): God gave us eternal life, and this life is in His Son. **12**He who possesses the Son has that life; he who does not possess the Son of God does not have that life. **13**I write this to you who believe in (adhere to, trust in, and rely on) the name of the Son of God [in the peculiar services and blessings conferred by Him on men], so that you may know [with settled and absolute knowledge] that you [already] have life, yes, eternal life. 1Jn 5:10-13
There is a sin that a Christian can commit that leads to death. (See also Heb 6:4-6)	If anyone sees his brother [believer] committing a sin that does not [lead to] death (the extinguishing of life), he will pray and [God] will give him life [yes, He will grant life to all those whose sin is not one leading to death]. There is a sin [that leads] to death; I do not say that one should pray for that. 1Jn 5:16

Perverting grace to allow sinful living, is to disown and deny our Lord Jesus. Though God saved the Israelites from Egypt, He later destroyed those of them who refused to adhere to, trust in and rely on Him. We are reminded that perverting grace to permit disobedience carries the same consequence today. Angels who were with God and *turned* from God, as well as the cities of Sodom and Gomorrah, serve as examples to warn us of everlasting fire if we *disown* Jesus with perverted grace. (See also 1Cor 10:5-12 & Heb 4:11)	4 For certain men have secretly slipped in among you – men who long ago were marked out for the condemnation I am about to describe – ungodly men who have turned the grace of our God into a license for evil and who deny our only Master and Lord, Jesus Christ. 5 Now I desire to remind you (even though you have been fully informed of these facts once for all) that Jesus, having saved the people out of the land of Egypt, later destroyed those who did not believe. 6 You also know that the angels who did not keep within their proper domain but abandoned their own place of residence, he has kept in eternal chains in utter darkness, locked up for the judgment of the great Day. 7 So also Sodom and Gomorrah and the neighboring towns, since they indulged in sexual immorality and pursued unnatural desire in a way similar to these angels, are now displayed as an example by suffering the punishment of eternal fire. 8 Yet these men, as a result of their dreams, defile the flesh, reject authority, and insult the glorious ones. Jude 1:4-8 NET
The Lord promises the crown of life to those who love Him. But there is a condition. Endurance. (See Rev 3:11 and James 1:12)	...Be faithful until death, and I will give you the crown of life. Rev 2:10, NKJV

Death is still a possible end for a believer if he doesn't wake up. Repentance is an ongoing choice. Choosing to stop obeying is choosing to receive Jesus as a thief rather than as a savior.	2 Wake up then, and strengthen what remains that was about to die, because I have not found your deeds complete in the sight of my God. 3 Therefore, remember what you received and heard, and obey it, and repent. If you do not wake up, I will come like a thief, and you will never know at what hour I will come against you. Rev 3:2-3 NET
The possibility of names being removed from the book of life is consistent with the rest of Scripture. (See Rev 17:8 and Ps 69:28)	Thus shall he who conquers (is victorious) be clad in white garments, and I will not erase or blot out his name from the Book of Life; I will acknowledge him [as Mine] and I will confess his name openly before My Father and before His angels. Rev 3:5
The Lord promises the crown of life to those who love Him. But it can be stolen if we don't endure. (See Rev 2:10 and James 1:12)	Behold, I am coming quickly! *Hold fast* what you have, that no one may take your crown. Rev 3:11, NKJV
Being lukewarm is like standing at the very edge of a cliff, sure to fall off if you died just then, for you would be spit out of Christ's mouth. Yet, still alive on the cliff, you are dearly and tenderly loved, and called to repent before it's too late.	15 'I know your deeds, that you are neither cold nor hot. I wish you were either cold or hot! 16 So because you are lukewarm, and neither hot nor cold, I am going to vomit you out of my mouth! 19 All those I love, I rebuke and discipline. So be earnest and repent! Rev 3:15-16,19 NET

Some people explain the erasures from the book of life by saying that we all start out in the book of life and then most get erased along the way. However, from this verse it is clear that not everyone starts out with his name in the book of life. (See Ps 69:28 and Rev 3:5)	The beast you saw was, and is not, but is about to come up from the abyss and then go to destruction. The inhabitants of the earth – all those whose names have not been written in the book of life since the foundation of the world – will be astounded when they see that the beast was, and is not, but is to come. Rev 17:8 NET
People who once had a share in the tree of life and the city of holiness, lose their share if they change the book of Revelation.	And if anyone takes away from the words of this book of prophecy, God will take away his share in the tree of life and in the holy city that are described in this book. Rev 22:19 NET

Appendix D

A TREASURE CHEST OF
EXCELLENT RESOURCES

We wouldn't want to keep all the best resources for ourselves! Here's a short list of some of the best we've found to propel growth in our own walk with God and in those whom we disciple. Be stimulated and inspired to grow in fruitfulness!

The NET Bible (Online at NetBible.org)
Download the whole Bible for free! The NET Bible was completed by experts in the original biblical languages who worked directly from the best currently available Hebrew, Aramaic, and Greek texts. The translators' notes make the original languages far more accessible. At Bible.org you can also access the largest Bible study resource on the Internet with over 40,000 pages of Bible study materials currently available.

The Visual Bible – Gospel of Matthew on Screen (DVD)
The book of Matthew dramatized word for word using the New International Version of the Bible. The depiction of Jesus seems inspired as Christ's character of love and truth is revealed on screen.

Affabel (CD)
An amazing audio drama produced in Hollywood by Christian author John Bevere. It's like watching something on the big screen, even though

it's in audio with all the big sounds and effects. This story puts the fear of God into you.

Bible 101 (Online at GoodSeed.com)
Free online video course offering a fantastic overview of the Bible starting in Genesis. It brings all the bits and pieces of a person's Bible knowledge together in one easy to see picture! This award-winning course sets you up to feed yourself from the Word with confidence like never before! (Also available on DVD as The Stranger On the Road to Emmaus.)

Good Person Test as an Animated Cartoon (YouTube)
A funny, thought provoking YouTube flick that gets the message across in a way you can send to anyone! Produced by The Way of the Master.

Hell's Best Kept Secret
Ever wondered why 90% of those making decisions for Christ are backsliding? This powerful message is worth listening to ten times or more! Listen at: thewayofthemaster.com.

The Way of the Master Basic Training Course
Many books and courses have tried, but this is the best I've ever seen to inspire and equip us to share our faith! It has revolutionized our ability to fish for men as a daily way of life!

Under Cover
This DVD series by John Bevere has convicted us and forever changed our lives and our view of the authorities God has put into our lives. It's so good and so foundational, it would revolutionize most churches if its message was taken to heart.

NCMI.net
A wealth of messages is available here online done by people who believe the whole Bible and aim to apply it by the power of God's Spirit.

23 Minutes in Hell (Book, DVD and YouTube)
Bill Wiese tells of his full sensory vision of hell where Jesus enabled him to experience hell as if an unbeliever. Like Paul the apostle said,

"Whether in the body or out of the body I do not know," but it was as if he'd been in heaven for real. Many people don't believe in a real hell. For this reason, Christ gave Bill a twenty-three minute taste of what the Bible describes.

A Shocking Message to Youth by Paul Washer
Paul grips the attention of today's youth with a message they aren't used to hearing! This message has gone viral on the Internet after 5000 youth were stunned with it live in the US.

Carman (Powerful Music with Powerful Messages Bursting with God and Creative Style)
This man of God is a rare catch, a singer song writer capable of the widest variety of music styles while packing a powerful biblical punch as a preacher through His songs. Carman is no common Christian entertainer. He's a man in love with Jesus and in gear to reach the lost and encourage the saints in almost any music style you can think of.

Keith Green (A Music Minister with Hunger for God Like Few Others)
Put a knife into Keith's music and it will bleed with a passion for God and a passion for the lost like few others. This man knew eternity is long and time is short. His impact was huge though he lived only a short life as a Christian before the Lord took him home.

Messages from Heaven (DVD)
A biblical examination of the apparitions of the Virgin Mary in the end times. This is produced by eternal-productions.org. and is available in a variety of languages.